A JOURNEY
INTO
VALUE SYSTEMS

CRACKING THE
GENIUS CODE

KEITH REGINALD THOMPSON

BALBOA.PRESS

A DIVISION OF HAY HOUSE

Balboa Press books may be ordered through booksellers or by contacting:

Balboa Press
A Division of Hay House
1663 Liberty Drive
Bloomington, IN 47403
www.balboapress.com
1 (877) 407-4847

ISBN: 978-1-9822-4170-4 (sc)
ISBN: 978-1-9822-4171-1 (e)

Library of Congress Control Number: 2020901108

Print information available on the last page.

Balboa Press rev. date: 01/24/2020

CONTENTS

A SHORT STORY OF MY PATH

I remember standing on the street corner near my home one day when I was thirteen years old. A voice came into my head and asked me, "Do you want to live as a good person or a bad person?" Even then I thought what a strange question that was to be popping into my head. Well, I announced I wanted to live as a good person.

Looking back to that time now that I'm an adult, I remember childhood experiences I had before I heard the good-life-or-bad-life question. When I was twelve years old, my mom wanted to search for a new life. She divorced my father when I was six years old. Our new life involved moving from Seattle, Washington, to Hampton, Virginia. My mother's family lived in Hampton. Upon arriving, we moved in with my Aunt Ester. She lived in a two-bedroom apartment in the projects called Pleasant Manor, a low-income residential area that was predominantly occupied by black American residents.

In doing a life review, I realize that I was at an impressionable age. In the 1960s, Virginia was a deep Southern state. I remember a stranger telling me I couldn't go down a certain street because KKK members lived down there. I remembered wondering, *What's a KKK?* I knew by the way the guy shared this information that it wasn't something good for me.

When it was time for me to attend school, my mom and Aunt Ester decided I would go to a predominantly white American school instead of a predominantly black American school. Four black kids went to Thorpe Junior High that year. It was a culture shock for me, and I'm sure it was for the white kids too! I don't know about the other black kids who went to Thorpe, but I wasn't treated nicely at all! I knew it had something to do with the color of my skin. I remember thinking why, because I had come from a diverse area in Seattle, even during that period in the 1960s.

I didn't connect with the school, the teachers, or my classmates. I didn't want to go to school, and my grades showed my unhappiness. I was in the school marching band and played the alto saxophone. To this day, I still love the sax!

Pleasant Manor was an interesting training ground for me. The first girl I was very interested in lived in Pleasant Manor. We were friends and always happy to see each other. I developed the art of playing marbles, which I enjoyed. I also honed my skills at playing basketball and was a much-improved player when I got back to Seattle.

On the flip side, Pleasant Manor was a war zone. There were lots of fights. It seemed as if everyone was fighting. I saw a man get shot; he was bleeding from his chest. That was the first time I had seen a man get shot. He was laboring for his life as he sat in a police car. They didn't have a medic on duty in those days. During one of the fights I witnessed, a boy was sliced across his left eye with a razor blade. That was going to make a permanent scar; you could tell by the way the injury would heal. I was always getting my butt kicked and felt disadvantaged because I wore glasses and had to take them off before they were demolished.

It was less than a year before my mom decided to move out of Hampton and back to Seattle. I asked her why she decided to move back to Seattle; she said, "Because I got tired of living in poverty."

When you are removing your ego emotions out of your past, you see a much clearer picture of your life.

—Keith Thompson

If I had chosen the bad life, I have to wonder if I would have reflected the violence I saw when I was living in Hampton. I can see how that experience played a role in my development. Have you ever felt as if there's a guide helping you along in your life experiences? Being asked if you want to live a good life or a bad life is a guiding question. I encourage everyone to look for those guiding questions throughout his or her journey.

In high school, I wasn't much into academics. My value systems in school were all about socializing, physical sports activities, doing enough homework to get by, and eating cinnamon rolls in the morning at school. Man, they had the best cinnamon rolls back then! I did have a job working for Dick's Drive-In flipping hamburgers. I was learning how to pave my way. I did graduate from high school. I was never encouraged to go to college by my parents. However, I was encouraged by my mother and father to go to work and learn a trade.

When I was nineteen, I started to work for Boeing Aerospace in Seattle. My father got me that job, and that was one of the best things he ever did for me. He was a supervisor there at that time. I ended up working for Boeing for twenty-eight years. I had a good career at Boeing. I wore many hats. I started as a mechanic and moved on to hand finisher, machinist, numerical control programmer, tool designer, lean manufacturer manager, and then manufacturing engineer. I took many classes at community colleges to obtain some of these positions. However, I can look back on my life and see that the work at Boeing wasn't my true passion. I was doing what I was conditioned to do. You see, my grandfather worked at Boeing, my father worked there, my mother worked there, I worked there, and yes, my oldest son worked there too!

While I was still living at home, I picked up a book I found in the garage called *The Power of Your Subconscious Mind* by Joseph Murphy. My mother had brought some books on positive thinking in her attempt to make some life improvements. The books ended up in the garage. When I saw the books, that familiar voice in my head said, "Pick up the books and read them."

In high school, I was never big into reading. I know now it was because I wasn't interested in the information in my school books. I not only read Joseph Murphy's entire book. I read *The Power of Your Subconscious Mind* three times. The information about the subconscious mind intrigued and inspired me. The subconscious mind was a topic not talked about in high schools. I had a strange but familiar attraction to this subject. It was as if I knew this information even though I hadn't read about the subconscious mind. *The Power of Your Subconscious Mind* was an introduction to the conscious and subconscious minds and an invitation for me to believe in myself. The knowledge from this book was the beginning process I needed to remember how the subconscious mind works.

"Know that in your deeper mind are Infinite Intelligence and Infinite Power" (Murphy 1962, 71).

I started reading all the books I could get my hands on by psychologists and doctors on self-help subjects, meditation, and metaphysical topics. I have a strong interest in the metaphysical. For insight for men, Dr. Herb Goldberg was my favorite author. I read all the material I could find on Edgar Cayce and took meditation courses and a dream analysis course from the Association for Research and Enlightenment (ARE). Mark Thurston, PhD, was a favorite of mine. His work helped me understand meditation and dream analysis. Other books I read three or more times were *Life and Teachings of the*

Masters of the Far East by Baird Spalding and *A Course in Miracles*. Interestingly, *A Course in Miracles* was published without an author name when it first came out. However, Helen Schucman wrote this wonderful book.

In 1974, I started to study martial arts, particularly Shorin-Ryu karate. Two guys who worked at Boeing in my group studied this style of karate. They showed me some cool techniques they'd learned, and that impressed me. I had always wanted to learn how to fight and protect myself, and that went back to my days at Pleasant Manor.

My black belt rank ended at the fourth-degree. I got out of the belt system and started working out on my own. I love to work out in nature. One of my favorite places to practice is by a river and anywhere where there are lots of trees. I am still a practicing student today.

In 1978, I went to the Washington School of Professional Hypnosis and became a certified clinical hypnotherapist. I wanted to know more about the conscious, subconscious, and super-conscious minds. I now call the super-conscious mind the higher mind. Reading *The Power of the Subconscious Mind* had exposed me to using self-hypnosis techniques to go within and quiet my mind. I wanted to help people to overcome challenging issues like cigarette smoking and weight problems. I started my hypnotherapy business and called it Inner World. I helped people with smoking, weight management, and past-life regression. Working with people in past-life regression was the interesting part. The goal was to find out why illness or challenging situations took place in people's lives and why major incidents happened in their lives. Understanding the initial cause is the principle I use today.

One woman client came to me twice for therapy. She was an obese woman, and she had tried everything to lose weight. We went through a past-life regression to review when the weight issues first occurred. We ended up in Egypt; the time frame was unclear. The king at the time would go to the villages to take the young girls to become part of his harem. She didn't want to go. She began to stuff herself with food, and she became obese. When it came time for the pharaoh to make his selections, he would not accept her. She carried her obesity behavior into this life realm to deal with her out-of-balance health values.

I got a call from a gentleman one day. He had recently been in a severe car accident and was paralyzed from the waist down. He wanted to know why he was experiencing paralysis. He was bound to a wheelchair and wanted me to visit him for hypnotherapy. I went to visit him a week later. This man was in his thirties at the time. So, we went back in time. We went back to the late 1300s where he was a high leader in Peru. I remember watching his mannerisms changing. He wasn't a nice leader. If anyone disobeyed him, he would have the person's leg cut off. He was laughing as he watched people hobbling away.

We make decisions, and our decisions impact who we are and how our personalities affect other people. There were millions of different decisions these two people could have made to prevent karmic patterns like these to carry over into present life realms. It has been my observation that we don't easily escape from what we create. The karmic payback could happen in another life realm.

I want to note that, when I had my private practice, I used the term *past life regression* to describe taking someone back in time. I have since changed that and now call it *life review*. It's a change in my understanding about time. I understand now that we can move backward and forward in time. We can look back in time to review what has happened, and we can look forward to seeing what could happen if we move forward with the same associated thoughts and beliefs we hold today.

I left Boeing in 2000 and got a divorce in 2003. During this period, I started rediscovering my passions. This time I started learning from top motivational and inspirational speakers. In 2006, I created my first talk show radio program at KKNW and Contact Talk Radio in Seattle: *Designing your Mind* with Keith Thompson. It was there that I started to find my voice. I created about eighty-five shows about the power of the mind. In 2007, I obtained certification as a professional health coach and created a course called Designing your Mind for Health. I had moderate success with this course, but it never caught fire. One of the cool things about this course was that people were losing five to ten pounds without adding any physical activities.

During this period, I learned about value systems. There are eight of them: Career and Personal Development, Emotional, Family, Financial, Health, Physical, Social, Spiritual. When I first started defining my value systems, I was confused about what my values were in any of the value systems. Few people were talking about defining what their values were. To help me with this problem, I developed the value of time exercise. That encouraged me to look at where I was spending all my time and on what value systems I was focusing at that time. The value of time exercise helped me see whether my job was contributing to my career and personal development or if my job was a financial value or both. When it came to eating, I had to look at my belief system about how I ate. Was I eating for health values, or was I eating to satisfy a craving? Did I want to satisfy hunger? That could be physical value.

I've studied Dr. John Demartini's work on value systems. He has defined seven major values, and in the journey, I added one more value to the journey, and that was health values. I pulled health values out of the physical values to give health a target focus.

I decided that, if I were to build another course, I would include all of the value systems; thus, here is *A Journey into Value Systems: Cracking the Genius Code.* I'm in gratitude to everyone who has given me valuable lessons.

I want to give special thanks to my mother, Celestine Elizabeth Harris. She has been my challenger and my supporter. Thanks mom!

Keith Reginald Thompson

CHAPTER 1

Introduction to A Journey into Value Systems

The Value Systems

"You are greater than you think you are!" These are the words I heard the first time I saw Mark Hughes, the founder of Herbalife, on stage in 1999. He repeated these words—"You are greater than you think you are"—three times. I figured that, if he took the time to repeat his message three times, he must mean it. I took the time and thought about his message. I wondered, *How do I move into this greatness?*

Looking back, I remember that, during my last years at Boeing, I wanted to do more with my life. At the time, I had worked at Boeing for over twenty-seven years. I'd had a good life and had made good money. I was starting to realize that working at Boeing and being an engineer wasn't my passion. I was at that age when I felt, if I don't do my passion now, I will never do it in this life. Helping others is my passion along with sharing information about how the mind works. I wanted something different in my life. I was into martial arts, health, and nutrition. I decided to start a Herbalife business.

To hear great speakers like Mark Hughes and Jim Rohn, Herbalife associates had to be at the supervisor level as distributors and travel to Orlando, Florida. Mark spoke in front of about eighteen thousand people from around the world. People came from Japan, all the European countries, Brazil, Mexico, Chile. Representatives from all of these countries were waving their national flags proudly. It was quite a sight to see.

Herbalife presented positive messages in its business structure that intrigued me. I met Jim Rohn at that same seminar, and he was inspirational. He was a motivational, inspirational, and transformational spokesperson for Herbalife.

"If you don't design your life plan, chances are you'll fall into someone else's plan. And guess what they have planned for you? Not much!" (Rohn, Good Read 2019).

I realized that, because I worked at Boeing, someone else had been planning my life for forty plus hours a week. I left Boeing a year later after hearing Mark and Jim in Orlando. I stayed with Herbalife for three years and left after Mark passed away.

The experience with Mark sparked me to listen and visit other great and inspiring speakers. I've met, read their books, and listened to many genius men and women from early 2000 to the present. In 2004, I met Dr. John DeMartini at one of his Breakthrough Experience seminars. He played a key role in helping me understand value systems.

"Until you value yourself, you can't expect anyone else to do so" (Demartini 2019).

This quote is the road to your greater self, and it's a road that never ends unless you choose to leave it and start demeaning yourself. A cool way to value yourself is to look at what you value about yourself. For example, are you respected in your relationships with people? Understanding how you want to be treated by others, including family members, is a great place to begin to build a genius value system. The journey into your value systems is about organizing your valued principles by placing what you value into groups. The value system groups are

- Career and Personal Development
- Emotional and Mental
- Family
- Financial
- Health
- Physical
- Social
- Spiritual

I had no idea what my values were in any of the value systems listed in this workbook. Many times, I was left confused and surprised by all the unsupported belief systems I had about myself. For example: I am having confidence in doing something great for the world and creating my world with financial abundance.

When you find an unsupported belief about yourself, that is the time to celebrate. Reward yourself with a big loud *yes!* or a high-five with someone or give yourself a big hug. The unsupported beliefs about yourself are causing chaos in your life and our world. In a nutshell, having unsupported beliefs about ourselves is ego mind driven and should be eradicated immediately. Understanding your value systems in a genius way refers to knowing your greatness, loving who you are, and loving our planet.

As I developed, I found both positive and negative belief systems in all my value systems. Understanding and redefining our values becomes transformational. By the time I complete writing this workbook, I will have studied my value systems for about sixteen years. I'll use martial arts terminology: It took me sixteen years to become a first-degree black belt in value systems. There are ten degrees in most martial arts systems that must be completed before a practitioner becomes master. Redefining my value systems is the journey I will stay on until I've mastered it. You might ask, how will you know when you've mastered it? My answer is when I am living every moment with my highest excitement.

Highest excitement is doing anything that drives your passion into who you want to be and what you want to experience at that moment. It can be anything from reading a good book to taking a trip to an unknown land and being on a spiritual quest. Your excitements can be in helping others live better lives or being in deep meditation experiencing oneness.

It has been my observation that, by introducing genius value systems to bring in higher standards of living, I have improved my life tremendously.

You'll see why some value systems are thriving and why other value systems are challenging. You now have the tools to remove any challenging value systems and turn them into a genius lifestyle.

CRACKING THE GENIUS CODE

Cracking the genius code is cracking *your* genius code. You do not have to develop the geniuses you are from scratch. You need to remember that the genius you are exists because of who we are.

According to the Merriam-Webster dictionary, one of the meanings of *genius* is "Extraordinary intellectual power especially as manifested in creative activity" (https://www.merriam-webster.com).

Viyahta, a blogtalkradio.com host, interviewed me on one of her programs, and we were talking about geniuses. All of a sudden, she blurted, "Out of the womb of a mother a genius is born!" Just imagine, a mother and a father realizing the genius of a future baby at conception and what a brilliant person he or she will be.

"Everyone is a Genius … But if you judge a fish by its ability to climb a tree, it will live its whole life believing it is stupid" (Einstein 2016).

I want to add, if you judge the fish on its ability to swim, the fish will be a genius.

Albert Einstein's point that we are all geniuses means we all have genius minds. To find our geniuses is to discover our uniqueness. We find our uniqueness by discovering our highest excitements in our value systems. Cracking the genius code means that we will be exploring our genius in each value systems.

What I'm asking all of my readers to do is to find their genius in all of the value systems as an organizing principle with their creativity. There are many geniuses in music, sports, theater, medicine, and the list goes on. However, a financial genius may lack skills in family dynamics or have completely ignored his or her health values and become ill. We have seen many times brilliant musicians fall prey to alcohol and drug abuse. This program helps you organize your value systems by looking at them from a genius perspective.

I wrote earlier about visiting and studying inspiring speakers. I named a few of them. There is one thing that all the speakers I visited had in common. They asked all the people in the audience to announce their genius: "I am a genius, and I have a genius mind." We would turn to the people around us and announce their genius: "You are a genius, and you have a genius mind."

Being a clinical hypnotherapist, I was struck with curiosity because I wanted to know how I could become that genius I had just announced. I knew it would take more than just saying it. I knew it would be a discovery process—but how?

Exploring our geniuses within the value systems is best done through the awareness of our thoughts, feelings, emotions, and beliefs. As you go about your daily routine, become aware of when you're using your genius mind and when you are using your ego mind. At the conscious mind level, it is impossible to use them both at the same time. However, within the subconscious mind, both the genius mind and the ego mind can be operating at the same time. If there's confusion as to why goals aren't manifesting, chances are the ego mind has a role in the process.

When you've completed the emotions of the genius and the ego mind exercise, you'll quickly see when you're using the genius mind and when you're using the ego mind in your decision making. Being aware of your emotions will help guide you in understanding and finding belief systems and where your values are. Discard every belief system that no longer serve a purpose for you and create new genius belief systems that serve you and others.

The geniuses come into play through your value systems to create organizing principles in your life. You'll notice synchronicities happening in your life. You'll begin to see the association between your thoughts, emotions, and belief systems with your physical world and your physical body. You'll see events happening rapidly.

Five things to consider cracking the genius code:

1. When you define your new value systems at the genius level, you are honing into your new genius lifestyle.
2. When being the observer, make sure you're in a balanced state of mind with no emotions. The universe is balanced. When we are the observers, we see the clearest path to take out of many choices. If you're having challenges in your life, being the observer is a great way to recognize emotions. We'll talk more about the observer.
3. Meditators will have the advantage. Meditation is all about going within the self. What's going on within the self (spiritual values) is the same as what's going on outside the self (physical values). By going within, you're able to reach higher levels of mind. It becomes much easier to fix challenging moments when they arrive.
4. Get to know your subconscious mind. Get to know your higher mind. Get to know your spirit using your genius mind. What does *spirit* desire to experience?
5. Mental focus is important. Know what your genius objectives are and stay true to them. When old behaviors, thoughts, emotions, and belief systems surface, stop them immediately and put them up for review by being the observer.

THE WORKBOOK

A Journey into Value Systems: Cracking the Genius Code is a workbook. It is your journey. The workbook is a personal journey in understanding life by understanding your value systems, emotions, and belief systems using your genius mind to organize your life.

The journey you will be taking is uniquely yours. Only you can take this journey, and no two journeys are exactly alike. There are many levels to this journey. How deep you go on your journey depends on how detailed you want to define and discover your value systems and find your genius in each of the value systems. The clearer your visions are about your value systems, the faster the results!

The workbook format of *A Journey into Value Systems* will enable you to get involved in the process. Writing things down is a way of setting events in motion. I hear all the time how much things have changed for the journeyers in a few months after they re-read their workbook. You can add information to your workbook at any time. There will be a period during which a particular value system demands a lot of attention. Use your workbook to define clear pathways to enhance powerful events or to remove challenging events in a value system.

If you are a first-time journeyer, I recommend that you scan the workbook, pay attention, and take mental note about what jumps out at you.

Next, I recommend that you do the sections of the workbook in order. In this way, you will get a complete feeling for the workbook and how it applies to your life. It's challenging to answer every single question the second time through. No worries! Keep going and allow the discovery and refining processes to begin.

This life coaching workbook is a key to unlocking the doors to your higher awareness. This workbook is a tool you can use to make definite changes in your life.

The workbook will assist in organizing your values, bring in awareness to your belief systems, and help you discover and announce your geniuses. Understanding what we value and how we are spending our time and money are the keys to making important changes in our lives. After doing the time study, find out what value systems are taking up the bulk of the day. It is important to know where you are so you can move ahead and live a life of excitements and passion.

Once you've become familiar with the workbook, feel free to move around the workbook to problem-solve issues. You can work on one specific value system to create a genius path. If you want to enhance your financial value systems, for example, you will use sections from the workbook like Defining your Genius Value System (financial values), the Value of Money, Understanding your Parents' Values (family values), the Emotional Balancing System, and Things I Desire.

A Journey into Value Systems **workbook explores:**

+ Organizing your genius value systems
+ Understanding the use of time within your value systems
+ Understanding the use of money within your value systems
+ Getting to know what life excitements are and creating new and exciting directions
+ Creating and implementing your desires
+ Understanding and recognizing the genius mind and the ego mind
+ Understanding your parents' value systems
+ Learning to balance your emotions
+ Exploring your methods of healing

EIGHT DIFFERENT VALUE SYSTEMS

+ **Personal Development and Career**

Personal development means using all your value systems in your own unique and genius way. Personal development is an evolving process. "I am greater than I think I am" is a great affirmation to use anytime.

Some paths to explore:

- Establish a genius personal and professional life path.
- Establish a new lifestyle in how you spend your time.
- Remove any negative emotions blocking your goals and objectives.

+ **Emotional and Mental**

Emotional refers to feelings that have reached their peak. Mental refers to an attitude about what you're experiencing or a frame of mind you want to set. Emotional values can lead you to what your beliefs are and what your thoughts are. You can do this by just asking questions like: Why am I feeling this way? What do I believe is true about this emotion? What thoughts are generating these emotions?

Establish high-vibrating emotions like happiness in all your value systems. Develop your mental attitude in all your value systems. For example, I have a warrior attitude when I practice martial arts. This warrior's attitude is part of all my value systems. My warrior health values are to eat healthy and nutritious foods. My warrior mentality is to protect my finances and to protect my family. Be sure to develop a mental attitude throughout your value systems.

Some paths to explore:

- Establish genius emotional values.
- Learn how to remove unwanted emotions and transform them into genius emotions.
- Learn how to be the observer of emotions and the results you are receiving.

✦ Family

Family plays a role in all the value systems. Family values come from the early programming and belief systems located in the subconscious mind for all the value systems. What we feel about wealth and finances, health, physical, social, spiritual, personal development and career direction, emotional and mental attitude all begins at family values.

Some paths to explore:

- Establish a genius family value system.
- Understand your family dynamics by being the observer.
- Heal out-of-balance relationships with family members through love and understanding.
- Establish new boundaries with family members by creating new belief systems.
- Learn how to remove old belief systems handed down by family members that are no longer needed.

✦ Financial and Wealth

Financial and Wealth values play a role in every value system, and you can build a financial umbrella under all your value systems. With the health value, you may want healthcare for you and your family. With the physical value, you may want to fill your environment with wonderful and beautiful material things. With emotional values, you want to create strong and positive energy-supporting finances and wealth. You can do this by creating powerful affirmations and belief systems.

Some paths to explore:

- Establish genius financial and wealth values.
- Remove emotional roadblocks and beliefs dealing with finances and wealth.
- Create a desirable financial lifestyle.

+ **Health**

Without our health, we can forget about enjoying any of our value systems. Our physical and emotional health is crucial in having a wealth filled life. Health and wealth are supportive of each other. I have seen many people who have been financially successful and missed the boat on health wealth.

Some paths to explore:

- Establish your genius healthy lifestyle.
- Discover causes of health issues.
- Establish paths to heal mental and physical health issues.

+ **Physical**

The physical value system is about our environment and the energy level of our bodies. The way you show up physically in your social environment plays an important role. It tells your social group and family members about the energy level of your mind-body. Like the other value systems, physical values show up everywhere. Consciously bringing symbols into your home can represent many of your values. For example, crosses that support your spiritual values can become strong energy magnets in your home. I like crystals. Bringing high-vibrating and colorful foods home from the grocery store will support health values.

Some paths to explore:

- Establish your genius physical lifestyle.
- Connect body and mind relationships.
- Learn about your environment.

+ **Social**

The social value system brings all your views to the forefront. It's that part of us that we share with others. Social values are about communicating how we view the world and life. Social values discuss how we display our emotions and our family values, how we judge ourselves and others, our spiritual values, and the company we choose to keep.

Some paths to explore:

- Establish your genius social lifestyle.
- Learn to heal out-of-balance relationships.

+ **Spiritual**

Your spiritual being is a combination of how you feel about all your values. The meaning of the word *spiritual* in *A Journey into Value Systems* is that we are all spirit (spirit-u-all). Under spiritual values, many people include their religious values. Spiritual values is a good place for religion because religion addresses all value systems. In *A Journey into Value Systems*, it doesn't matter what religion you are. What matters is whether your religious viewpoints are operating from a perspective of genius or ego. You can quickly tell which it is by deciding whether or not you're embracing everyone or just a select few.

Some paths to explore:

- Establish your genius spiritual values.
- Explore your beliefs about life.

A Journey into Value Systems is a life mission to accomplish all your desires. Once you start, what you value will be an important part of your life. The study of the eight value systems will organize your life and give you the realization of how you're interacting with people around you and your physical realities. You'll begin to see what your family members' and friends' values are. Looking at our values from a genius perspective assures us we are on the right path. Creating desires along with our exciting lifestyle tells the Universe we are taking an active part in our lives, and the Universe responds to these types of activities.

A Journey into Value Systems: Cracking the Genius Code creates the alignment to all of your value systems. Defining your genius in each of your value systems creates the alignment to all your goals and desires.

Disclaimer

A Journey into Value Systems details my personal experiences with and opinions about value systems and how the mind works. This book is not intended to replace professional care in any of the value systems.

To get on my mailing list: myvaluesystems@gmail.com

Contact: Keith Thompson

Website: www.myvaluesystems.com

Enjoy the journey!

Keith Reginald Thompson

CHAPTER 2

CRACKING YOUR GENIUS CODE

I f you were to ask me if I believe in God, I would tell you yes. I will also tell you that the god I believe in isn't a supreme being outside of us and peering down on us. This supreme being is within each one of us. It is by going within through any form of meditation that we find our supreme being that has no limitations. The god I'm learning about goes well beyond being a supreme being and is the creator of All That Is! "All that is" means to me that everything that exists is God. Anything this God didn't create doesn't exist. It is impossible to exist and not be a part of this God's energy. This energy includes the highest vibrational frequency down to the lowest vibrational frequency. Even voids exist to give us the ability to go into the unknown to bring something new into existence. We have the ability to do this. Our genius abilities rest in this kind of activities. The easiest way to define voids is that they are something missing from our lives that we want to experience or to bring in new material or spiritual creations.

Because we are a part of the creative process and can create, we become responsible for what we are creating. There's no getting around this. Whatever we create and bring into existence has our signature on it.

I marvel at our genius scientists who build the spacecraft that travel as far as distant planets like Saturn and Uranus. We can now see our solar system and neighboring planets from a three-dimensional perspective. When I visit the NASA website, I am amazed at the splendor of our Universe. I know there are over billions or maybe even trillions of other galaxies in our Universe. I asked the question, "This is part of who we are?" The voice in my head replies, "Of course it is!"

On your journey, look for reasons to be amazed and see the splendor of who we are. "All that is" means there's no separation between us. It means we and everything we see around us is all one. We are the expression of the divine being some of us (Christians, Jews, and Muslims) call God! From our family members who sit at the dining table with us all the way to some remote galaxy billions of lightyears away, we are all one. What bridges the illusional gap between us is love.

There are billions of possibilities within each second we live. All we must do is be open to possibilities and explore our inner minds. Everything exists within the different levels of your inner mind. I use *inner mind* to mean the part of us we discover when we go within to unlock the doors to higher awareness. To go within starts with closing your eyes and focusing your attention on what you see and feel inside. Yes, we do see things when we close our eyes.

To operate through the genius mind means being connected to All That Is. Thought processes, emotions, and belief systems are tools of our genius minds. When you realize everything is connected, you open to the omniscient (all knowing), omnipotent (all powerful), omnipresent (present everywhere) universal laws, your soul, your spirit, your higher mind, your physical mind, and your physical body.

Omnipresent is our clue that God is in all things, and we are part of All That Is. Omniscient is our clue we have access to a wealth of knowledge. Omnipotent is our clue we are all powerful.

BRINGING YOUR GENIUS TO THE FOREFRONT

One of the most important discoveries we can make is to realize our genius. I look forward to the day when our public school systems support kids being geniuses and develop educational systems in which no child is left behind and every child develops a strong understanding of his or her values—social, financial, family, spiritual, physical, health, emotional, career and personal development.

The following discovery exercise is about finding your geniuses. Our genius minds can give something wonderful to the world. What is it you're good at and have passion for? If you were to develop your genius mind, what would you develop and bring into the world? Understanding which value systems are your strengths and which value systems are your challenges is an important step to cracking your genius code. Some people may have a strong financial value system and have a health value system that needs a lot of work. Knowing your values is the key to opening your geniuses, especially if you choose to be in alignment with All That Is.

The genius mind can transcend any shortcomings by understanding its connection to All That Is and using any of the knowledge that presents itself. Learning how to transform ego emotions into genius emotions is a worthy goal. With the genius mind, we can open the doors to everything we wish.

In our greatness, we all have something we can develop and bring it into reality.

To discover the depth of our gifts, we must believe in our gifts and begin the process of bringing the genius gifts into our world and to the planet. I am asking you in this exercise to open your heart— love—and bring in your greatness. Just by asking and answering the nine questions, the process of discovery will begin.

Daily, for about ten to twenty minutes, find a comfortable place to relax. Close your eyes and take in a couple of deep breaths to relax the body and mind. When your mind and body are in a relaxed state, use your feelings to begin the connection with your subconscious mind and higher mind. Ask the question, "What are my geniuses?" Confirm, "Higher mind brings my geniuses to my awareness." Look for connections with your higher mind and subconscious mind by feeling the connection and seeing images. I suggest doing this exercise for each question. Incorporate this type of work into your daily routine. You will notice a difference. As children, we had great imaginations. It is time to bring our spirits and higher minds back to play!

Sometimes we must look for our geniuses. Here are some places to explore. Talk to your friends about these questions. Keep all ego discussions out of the picture—negative stuff! Build on what you see (imagination) and feel (emotional excitement).

1. **Am I communicating with my imagination?**

_____

_____

2. **What do I love to read about?**

_____

_____

3. **Can I dedicate my life to a good cause?** _____ **If yes, what?**

_____

_____

4. **What am I passionate about?**

_____

_____

5. **Who are my mentors?**

_____

_____

6. **What are the things my friends and family members tell me I am good at?**

_____

_____

7. **What did I do as a child that was genius?**

_____

_____

8. **What are my geniuses?**

_____

_____

9. **If I were to create my genius, what value system(s) would it be in?**

_____

_____

One of the key points to realize is that we are individuals. Our uniqueness on Earth starts with our spirits, our higher minds, our physical minds, and our physical bodies. The following information is from my observation through practice, research, and life experiences. I encourage you to learn and remember all the different aspects of your *being*.

THE SPIRIT

When we realize we are a spirit (spiritual), we remember we are more than just a physical body. We move into what the spirit wants to experience in life. Spirit comes from a nonphysical place. Spirit plays to a higher order in the physical realm because spirit is beyond this world. When we announce "I am living my life by spirit" we are taking charge of our life's direction on Earth. Our physical bodies and physical minds operate to serve our spirits.

People who believe they are just a physical body may experience more challenges. They interpret most of their life experiences through their five physical senses. Many people who fall into this category fail to realize that there's a higher power that oversees everything. They see the world from outside looking in instead of from the inside looking out. In other words, seeing is believing instead of believing is seeing.

"The 'I' of you is not the physical body; that is simply an instrument which the 'I' uses to carry out its purposes; the 'I' cannot be the Mind, for the mind is simply another instrument which the 'I' uses with which to think, reason, and plan" (Haanel 1916, 16).

The pronoun *I* has a direct association with your spirit. When you say "I," your subconscious mind's hard drive is automatically turned on and it waits for the command that follows. For example: "I am happy, joyful, peaceful, and loving." You should avoid any negative "I" commands such as, "I can't," "I hate," "I won't," and similar commands, which move you into lower frequencies and limit your ability to create with your genius mind. Negative commands are considered ego mind creations in the journey.

Realizing that the pronoun *I* has a direct relationship with spirit and the subconscious mind, you now have the beginning tools to create genius concepts. For example; "I am a loving wife," "I am a brilliant musician," "I am healthy, wealthy, and wise," "I am emotionally balanced and intuitive," "I have lots of wonderful friends," and the list goes on and on. The attitude of gratitude plays a big role in acknowledging All That Is. It keeps us humble and in tune.

THE HIGHER MIND

The higher mind is also known as the superconscious mind, the divine mind, and Christ consciousness.

It is extremely important to develop awareness and form a relationship with your higher mind. Your higher mind has no space and time limitation. In other words, the higher mind is beyond this physical plane and not bounded by Earth's three-dimensional limitations of space and time. The higher mind contains the information about why you are here. People who can retrieve information from the Akashic records more than likely have an awareness of their higher minds.

The higher mind has a direct connection with your soul history. The soul history includes any Earth lifetimes and the purpose of each lifetime. I have seen these many times in my therapy work with clients. With the help of higher mind, we'll obtain a better understanding of the relationship we have with loved ones. We'll have a better understanding of karmic patterns in our value systems; for example, with health values. We can have a better understanding of karmic patterns and have fewer judgments of tragic situations. There are no emotions in the higher mind! All emotions stored in the subconscious mind are part of physical reality. In the two stories about past lives I included previously, the clients had access to their higher minds to bring in their valuable information that included their soul histories. The soul history information supported why one client was obese and the other client lived a life in a wheelchair. As I mentioned before, the higher mind is beyond space, time, and physical reality. One of the reasons that some people don't remember past lives is that the information isn't located in the physical subconscious mind. Many people have belief systems that past lives don't exist, and therefore, the information becomes blocked from entering the subconscious mind from the higher mind.

One of the ways the higher mind communicates is through the imagination. When we have daytime visions, the chances are that the higher mind is communicating. The subconscious mind records all information coming from the higher mind to review at any time. For example, when we create desires in life, the higher mind sends back images of how the desire may look. We can consciously assist the higher mind in the style of a new home we want, and higher mind will send back images to set things in motion. That's why sometimes we hear, "That's exactly the way I envisioned my house would look!" When the spirit part of us sets desires in the higher mind, it already exists because it is beyond space and time. All we must do is bring it into physical reality. The art of creation is to move the desire out of the invisible into the visible three-dimensional world. The conscious mind actions must not interfere with the higher mind and the subconscious mind. The main reason our desires do not manifest is because the ego mind sabotages the process with negative beliefs and emotions. The ego mind says, "You can't do it!" Stay the course of your desires and learn who you really are from the higher levels.

THE PHYSICAL MIND

The physical mind is be defined in *A Journey into Value Systems* as the level of mind to use in physical reality. The physical mind involves the subconscious mind and the conscious mind. There are thousands of books on the topic of the subconscious mind and the conscious mind. I am going to discuss how these two levels of the mind can best serve you in the journey.

THE SUBCONSCIOUS MIND

Your subconscious mind is the power center of your physical reality. The subconscious mind is involved in every process of dealing with your physical reality. This involvement includes the functioning of your body, brain, and physical mind. Your power center includes knowing everything happening in this life realm—past and present experiences and future direction. There are four key functions of the subconscious mind in the journey of cracking your genius code: belief systems, emotions, feelings, and current thought processes that represent past, present, and future realities

"It is through the subconscious that we relate to the Universal Mind and brought into relation with the Infinite constructive forces of the Universe" (Haanel 1916, 6).

- **Our belief systems:** Our belief systems are considered the top tier of the physical mind because there's nothing stronger than what we believe. Our belief systems are attached to emotions, feelings, and thought processes within the subconscious mind. Any beliefs within our subconscious mind become our physical reality. Every belief has an origin. The beliefs can be from parents, religion, school systems, television, social groups, and genetic coding from past generations. The beliefs we have can show up within the physical body and in our environment (physical values). Our beliefs play a major role in all our value systems. Our beliefs determine if we are living in abundance or lack. If we believe that money is the root of all evil, chances are pretty good that money will fly away from us, and we will have challenges obtaining and keeping money.

  Pay attention to the belief systems of your society. Do your value systems fit within the framework of your society? Do you know where you fit in with the movement of your nation or your planet? I don't mean that you must fit within groups; chances are that you already do. It's good to know where your beliefs are within a certain social structure. Many social structures attempt to form and develop your belief systems.

  A good example of this is religion. Your feelings will let you know if you're making the right connections.

  Politics create many belief systems in our society. Around the world, we see uproars meant to change the views of leaders or to remove them from control. Within these political structures, we see people who are thriving and people who live in suppression. Many of the collective agreements are shifting politics to a higher vibration in which more people are demanding a better way of life. As we develop firmer beliefs and value systems for ourselves, we are raising the vibration of our nations and the world. We all have a role in this process.

  Your subconscious mind takes everything you say literally. This literal action takes place when you are talking with someone or when you are alone deep in thought. The subconscious mind is subjective and follows the guidelines of your beliefs along with those of the people you are involved with, the places you go, and the emotions you display supporting those beliefs. That means that everything in the subconscious is the truth for your reality even if it's a lie in the overall scheme of things.

  Good examples of lies are fears that are not based on concrete evidence, any emotions that create disharmony, or judgments based on ego mind interpretations. Many people do not know what beliefs govern their value systems. Therefore, these people are subject to beliefs from outside information like tribal and family beliefs, news media propaganda from watching television (tell-a-vision), and not understanding how the body and mind work. We must learn how to be a good hosts to our minds and bodies. We do this by establishing genius belief systems and understanding our value systems.

  Your subconscious mind can use a good housecleaning to remove the lies that have become beliefs. A good housecleaning begins with becoming aware of your negative beliefs.

It's important to know when beliefs, emotions, feelings, and thought processes are no longer true for you. This understanding realizes that the genius mind and the ego mind belief systems operate at the same time in the subconscious mind. Genius and ego beliefs are the reasons that confusion and chaos exist in your mind and your life. The goal is to move into the genius mind realm of choices instead of operating in duality and from the ego mind perspective. We have this ability.

A genius belief creates a genius lifestyle; this requires planning. Planning doesn't have to be a big elaborate process. Find something to grow into and become. Now, you can plan out the direction you would like to take to get you there. This growth can take place in any of the value systems. Maybe it's becoming that author you always wanted to be or developing a beautiful mind and body that is full of love and light. Creating with the genius mind gives new and exciting direction and new belief systems to support your growth.

We hear all the time about creating a business mission statement for your business. How about creating mission statements for each of your value systems? Developing your mission statements in each of your value systems is a great way to start new belief systems that create your genius lifestyle. With your mission statements, you can aim for the highest values you have in each value systems. You can always adjust your values and mission statements as the growth continues. Developing mission statements and reasons for having genius value systems is a great way to establish new desires in your life.

There's one more thing I want to discuss in this section—you should connect with your higher power and develop a relationship with it. When you connect with your higher power, you get to know when the higher mind is communicating with your subconscious mind and genius mind. Make your life decisions from the spirit level instead of reacting to old behaviors, emotions, and beliefs. Reacting to old beliefs keeps the old beliefs and emotions in the present moment. Operate all of your life choices from spirit level. Operating from spirit level may mean you'll have to become someone else to move out of an unpleasant situation. When you hear this for the first time, you may find it surprising. Changing your beliefs will change your energy and change your personality. Additionally, your spirit, in the process, creates an alignment to a higher power instead of operating from old subconscious beliefs based on physical reality and the ego mind.

When faced with an unpleasant situation, announce, "I am creating a new situation." Now, start the process of creating a new life by creating alignment with your genius mind, subconscious mind, the higher mind, spirit, universal laws, omnipresent, omniscient, omnipotent. Announce what *you* choose to experience in *your* life. Remember when we use the word *I*, we draw the connection to spirit whether we know it or not.

There is a part of you that is beyond physical reality. Ask your higher mind for your soul history and gain the understanding of why you're here on Earth. Develop an understanding of your family members and why there's a connection among you. The goal here is to start connecting with your genius self and let that connection guide and inform you as you search for what you need to know and believe.

+ **Our emotions:** Anything we're emotional about is attached to belief systems. The emotions of past and future events operate in the subconscious mind. Our emotions are the filters we see in life. The emotion of fear is a good example of filters we see in a life governed by the ego mind. The question to ask is, what is it I choose to see in life? You can begin to find the answers by being aware of your emotions. Sometimes we hear someone talking about life say, "Everything just is!" This statement means there are no emotions in any situation unless we place them there. If we place judgment on any situation, that is the process of keeping a belief system alive or developing a new one.

All judgments attach themselves to an emotion! Let's say you tell yourself "I am fat and ugly," and you feel the emotion of guilt attached to this affirmation. The affirmation itself is an attack on the physical body. This affirmation also states this is what *you* (spirit) want to experience. The emotion of guilt is an attack on your mental attitude. This affirmation and others like it are destructive! The ego mind always has emotions to attack your mind and body or someone else's mind and body. The ego mind's function is to view all situations with negative energy and emotions. Your goal must be to avoid the ego mind's energy as much as possible, even if this means getting rid of certain beliefs and people in your life.

Become aware of who you are in your emotional values. See what emotions are popping up for you, especially around friends, family members, and your major value systems. Financial values are charged emotionally for many Americans. The emotionally charged energy may start in the financial values and move into health values based on associated belief systems. For example, a person with limited income may establish a belief system of "I can't afford organic foods" and limit himself to eating at McDonald's and other fast-food restaurants. In return, eating at fast-food restaurants could create health problems.

A person with unlimited income may have a belief system of eating only organic foods prepared by a hired chef. This person exercises along with eating healthy foods and may live a long and healthy life. Eventually, one emotion can influence all your value systems. If you excessively smoke cigarettes, drink alcohol, use recreational or pharmaceutical drugs, or overeat at mealtimes, discover what emotions are driving the events and what value system is the dominant player. If you like what you see, keep the emotion. If you don't like an emotion, stop the emotion and begin the process of replacing the old emotion with a genius emotion and belief system. Removing emotions can be challenging because emotions are life forces. The brain produces chemicals in the body called neuropeptides that connect to cell receptors in the body and bridge the gap between brain and body. There are chemical releases for every emotion. The emotions are accompanied by thought processes and belief systems as well. Please understand how powerful this can be when we use our genius minds. I believe our emotions can be used for health and used for treating illnesses.

From the genius mind perspective, the emotions are uplifting and inspiring (in spirit). Use your genius mind to build new emotional foundations for all your value systems to build a stronger foundation in your physical reality. In this workbook, you'll build your genius emotion list. Find reasons to use your genius emotions in all your value systems. Wake up energized developing your genius emotions. Use the energy of love to help assists you in your growing process. I'll talk more about the energy of love under Our Feelings.

One of the keys to solving the subconscious mind riddle is deciding what emotions you want to experience. Another key is getting rid of the emotions you don't want to experience. Removing old emotions, thoughts, and belief systems can be difficult mental work. It can take years to solve deep emotional trauma and change the energy into a genius emotion. It will be worth it!

"Emotions are chemical feedback, the end product of experiences we have in our external environment" (Dispenza 2019).

In some of Dr. Joe Dispenza's seminars, he discussed how emotions can run three generations deep through our genetic coding. He also discussed how the genetic switches can be turned on and off. If the emotions are the end product of our experiences and these genetic switches can turn on and off, we should pay more attention to our emotions. If our parents are passing down genetic codes through their genes, there can be subconscious memories within the codes. That means there are belief systems attached to these coding passed on by parents. I'm paying special attention to this because both my parents had cancer. My father lost his life to cancer, and my mother is a cancer survivor. One of the key factors here is that both my parents smoked cigarettes, and I do not. Here are two interesting facts: my father kept smoking cigarettes and lost his life, and my mother stopped and is an eighteen-year survivor of cancer.

When I was around seven years old, kids in the neighborhood had a cigarette club. We would bring in cigarettes from home and go to the basement, play music, and smoke. Back then, cigarettes were easy to obtain. A pack of cigarettes cost only thirty-five cents. With that amount of money and a note from home, we had cigarettes. We had plenty of notes on hand from our parents because we were able to keep the notes after we bought the cigarettes. I remember three main brands that we smoked: Salem, Kool, and Camel. I remember that Camels were gross and Salems tasted of menthol. My mom smoked Salems.

We were practicing being the product of our environment. We weren't displaying specific emotions, except we were trying to be cool as we experimented. However, when I look at my parents' lives, clearly I can see certain emotions they displayed. From my parents, the emotion of stress and the emotion of anger played big when I was a young boy. There's no judgment here as I'm telling this. Draw the connection from what is going on in your environment to what emotions are visibly displayed. Watching emotions is an eye-opener!

When you discover a negative emotion in your family lineage, start discharging the unwanted emotion immediately. Discover what the emotions are and decide what value systems the emotions are in, like family values. We want to move unwanted ego emotions into genius emotions. You are changing hate energy to love energy. I think we can turn our genetic switches on and off this way.

My mother and father had cancer at the same time and had surgery within one week of each other. My parents had been divorced for over thirty-eight years and had not seen each other. Do you think that got my attention? You bet it did!

Explore your genetic coding, especially if there's a specific illness in the environment; for example, cancer. Look for any ego mind emotions like anger and hatred toward someone. The energy level of these emotions is low in vibration and may play a role in the illness. Review the Emotional Balancing System.

+ **Our feelings:** I believe that feelings are the most underused tool we have. We know about feelings, and we recognize them when we experience them. However, are we using feelings to our advantage? Feelings are the energy that runs through all locations involved with your belief systems, attracting experiences. Feelings reinforce or dissolve belief systems. Therefore, the genius mind should be at the forefront of all your decisions. In its purest intent, feelings can transcend space and time. In other words, our feelings can connect to the higher mind. Feelings are the energy flowing in the physical mind from thoughts to emotions to beliefs and from beliefs to emotions to thoughts. In this two-way action, feelings can connect and retrieve information to our advantage. When we realize this energy, feelings become an extremely valuable tool for healing, living an abundant life, and seeing how we feel about the people and the world around us.

Feelings from thoughts to emotions to belief systems—the creative process

Whatever we create in our world usually starts with a thought. I'm sometimes amazed at how many people in our society are unaware of this fact. Thoughts are where many of the problems begin because we manifest what we don't want because we are unaware of our thinking power. Once a thought has begun, the feeling process is activated. This process doesn't care if you're using your genius thoughts or your ego thoughts.

When you're in the creative process, see the results of what you want to experience. All your thought processes should support the results. For example, make the statement or affirmation, "I am going to Egypt this fall." The result is the Egyptian trip. A person may feel excitement over this trip and begin to incorporate the emotional experience of joy and happiness while looking at pictures, seeing images in his or her mind, and planning the trip. This example shows how you can create reality in your mind with your thoughts and emotions before the events happen, which is the belief. Your subconscious mind records the whole process.

Feelings moving from emotions to belief systems are a little complex because, many times, we are dealing with belief systems and feelings of the past. We must create new belief systems to support new experiences. For example, someone who has been living on the streets for the last seven years wants to get off the streets and live a rewarding life. The new thoughts, feelings, and emotional processes will have to match the result of the rewarding lifestyle. At the same time, the person should start the process of denouncing the old belief systems and associated emotions. Feelings become a valuable tool because feelings show you what you are entertaining in thought and emotion. The feelings must match the new belief systems. The end results must be kept in mind as much as possible. If it isn't, things will not manifest in your favor, and the future will become challenges. Keep the feelings of fear and lack out of all your dreams and desires.

When we begin organizing our belief systems, beliefs become easier to work with using value systems. When planning trips, for example, we know financial values, social values, and family values may be involved. We can now develop genius value systems, like financial values, that are supportive of our new beliefs, emotions, thoughts, and desires. Now, we can move our feelings through a strong, cohesive network.

Feelings from belief systems to emotions to thoughts—the discovery processes

To grow, we must remove outdated belief systems that are in the way of our genius lifestyle, even if the belief system was handed down from our parents and grandparents. Belief systems formulated a hundred years ago may not apply in today's world. There will be situations where you'll ask the question, "What in the world created this?" If you're truly looking for the answer, the subconscious mind will respond. In the discovery process, ask lots of direct questions.

When a belief system reveals itself, the next question to ask is, "What are the associated emotions tied to this belief?" Sometimes emotions will reveal themselves first because they are the end result of an experience. Ask the question, "What are the associated belief systems attached to this emotion?" Fear (false emotions appearing real) is an emotion that easily can flow through all the value systems. Keep in mind that we are using our feelings to draw the connections between belief systems to emotions to thoughts. Feelings reveal other emotions and beliefs involved in a circumstance. Pay close attention to what thoughts are surfacing and what you're saying about the situation.

Next time you have a conversation with a friend or a family member, make note of where your feelings are taking you. Also, when you're alone and deep in your thoughts, observe your feelings. You'll begin to see if the feelings are genius driven or ego-driven. To discover emotions in friends and family dynamics is an eye-opener because they will reflect on you and affect your energy. Therefore, it's important to remove negative people out of your life. Entertainment of all unwanted feelings must stop. Or you must discuss them with those who bring them to remove them out of your physical reality.

Feelings can flow outside of physical reality. I haven't found any limitations on where feelings can go or what feelings can attract. We can feel our way into the unknown to explore our future desires. We can use our feelings to create dialogs with our higher minds and entertain our imagination. We can view our Akashic records with our feelings by communicating with our higher minds. Through feelings, we can create emotions for future experiences and develop excitement within genius emotions. When genius connections happen with the higher mind, entertain your feelings as far as you can with your imagination. You will be able to feel what your part is in All That Is, which is in the unknown and a continued discovery that never ends. All you must do is start the inquiry, feel the energy, explore the information you receive, and act on your excitement.

Being aware of your feelings when you are eating is a great way to tune into love energy. Turn off any background noises like television, negative music lyrics, or radio because of its unpredictable programming (like a negative news story). When we eat, we are putting energy into our bodies. If our feelings are positive and loving while we eat, we are bringing in beautiful energy into the body. If our feelings are negative while we eat, we risk the chance of bringing in lower vibrations to the body. If a person is ill, this would be one of the first questions I would ask him or her, "How do you feel while you are eating?" This question will lead to the feelings and emotions involved with the illness. If there are financial troubles or family issues, many people will take their troubles to the eating table. Avoid eating with negative feelings! When I was studying my clinical practice, we were studying weight issues. The teacher told us that over-weight issues arise from unresolved emotions that are stored in the body.

It is imperative that you explore your feelings within your body and environment. The question to ask yourself: "How do I feel about my body and my environment?" The environment is anyplace you may find yourself—the workplace, home, or a natural environment, such as the environment you might experience when going for a walk.

Here's an exercise for you. Pick a beautiful day—a day when you're in a good mood. Briefly look at the Sun and then close your eyes. (Note: This is not a stare-at-the-Sun exercise.) With your feelings, feel the Sun's energy and feel its source. The Sun has connected with you. Now go to the Sun and make a connection with it. When you finish with the connection, open your eyes. When you do this exercise and make the connection, remember that your feelings traveled ninety-three million miles in less than a second. By the way, you can do this exercise with all the planets in our solar system.

When we use our feelings with genius emotions and omniscience as a way of learning, they become a powerful tool.

If there are emotions you do not want, stop sending your feelings to those emotions. If you want to stop the emotion of anger toward another person, stop sending feelings to that emotion and that person. Anger emotions can be replaced with love emotions.

"Stop. Change. New direction." This is a command you can use whenever a recognized unwanted feeling wants to reconnect to an old belief system. The new direction will be defined when you do the genius value system exercises. Keep in mind that we are energy maintained by our subconscious minds. The brain is the switchboard that houses our energy on the physical level. The methods I'm prescribing are ways to take charge of this energy.

Your feelings have connections with your higher mind, your spirit, and your soul.

The expression "feel the love" is real!

THE CONSCIOUS MIND

The conscious mind is the director of the subconscious mind. The conscious mind is responsible for the duality we see between genius and ego. Good and evil can be compared to genius mind and ego mind. If you have an awareness of your spirit and choose to guard your mind by thinking thoughts that promote the highest and best for everyone, you will see vast improvements in your life.

The unaware person will accept thousands of suggestions from parents, friends, social media, news media, and television (tell-a-vision) programming into the subconscious mind. People who watch lots of television have lots of information in their subconscious minds that is not their thinking. Many people are unaware that a pharmaceutical drug commercial may influence their life. The message is that drugs are the method for curing illnesses. I'm convinced commercials by companies like Coke, Burger King, and Chevy cars and trucks, to name a few, all have influenced untrained minds. How about those "What's in your wallet?" credit card ads? The messages from these ads are running free-range in the subconscious minds of viewers, just waiting to be selected. The goal of commercials is for us to see products in the store, like Coke cans, for example, and then recall subconscious images of beautiful and happy people drinking Coke and having fun. The actual purchase of the product follows this brain association. Many of the tell-a-vision products are no good for us. Look for yourself and review how many television products are no good for us. It may surprise you.

"Every day, stand guard at the door of your mind" (Rohn, Top Results Academy 2019). This refers to the spirit overseeing and directing so that, when a person becomes spiritually awake, he or she is aware of his or her spirit. The conscious mind now becomes The Guardian at the Gate. The Guardian at the Gate refers to the protector of the subconscious mind and the creative process. The conscious mind is given the power to accept or reject ideas for the creative process. The conscious mind also has the power to accept or reject any past thoughts, emotions, or beliefs that are brought to its attention. The conscious mind can make the command "I no longer believe this" to change the experience of the event.

Remember that the subconscious mind accepts everything it is told to be true whether it is true or not true.

Spirit (spiritual values) can now create an alignment with the conscious mind and use the genius mind to create wonderful things to experience. Currently, Earth is a three-dimensional world, and this three-dimensional world involves duality. Duality from the journey perspective deals with using the genius mind or the ego mind in everything we experience in life. Being the observer is the neutral point of the genius mind and ego mind. The ego mind isn't just going to go away at this dimensional level because we are here to understand how to navigate through duality and move into oneness with All That Is. Many people who are unaware of their spirit will be operating from their ego minds with glimpses of genius awareness. To move into oneness with All That Is takes determination, desire, and focus on staying in alignment with the genius mind.

- **The thinker:** Because the conscious mind can think only one thought at a time, we are using either our genius mind, ego mind, or being the observer (no thought) in the thinking process at any given time. The genius mind and the ego mind do not work at the same time. However, we can have a genius thought at one moment and have a negative ego thought that contradicts the genius thought in the next moment. This type of thinking process confuses the subconscious mind and creates chaos in the creative process. A tremendous amount of care should be taken in the private thinking process (thinking when alone) and what you say aloud to someone else. Genius mind and ego mind thinking processes can create and manifest whether you are thinking aloud or silently. Define your desires as clearly as possible, without any doubts, and remove all negative emotions from the feeling process. Stop entertaining negative thoughts about yourself and others. The ego mind comes from a place of insanity and doesn't know it and doesn't care.

- **The genius mind:** The goal of the genius mind in the journey is more than creating brilliance in a field or trade. The genius mind brings into balance all our values and all our desires into oneness. The genius mind concept is the organizing principle that aligns us to the highest possibilities in this life. We are here on Earth for a short period. Many people have forgotten the reasons they are here. Aligning yourself with your genius mind brings in knowledge from the higher mind that is beyond space and time. You move into a knowingness that sometimes you can't explain. For example, you may realize that you're in a parallel reality where several events, from different perspectives, are happening at the same time. This can also manifest in visions and feelings of previous times on Earth or knowing that someone is watching you or thinking about you. I know this information may be mind blowing to some. Your soul can do some amazing things. Use the genius mind and create alignments with your subconscious mind and higher mind to assist being in your body and to navigate here on Earth. Use the ego mind, and you'll have no such alignment.

  Use your genius mind to bring in strong emotions to support your alignment with All That Is. When you are feeling the love energy, that is a powerful place to connect. When I learned that to love was not my creation, I was so relieved. I no longer felt I had to create the energy to love someone. All I must do is move into the energy of love with my feelings and send it to whomever I wanted to receive it. The love energy has a natural link to everyone by inheritance from All That Is. However, we can turn the love energy into an emotion. Love is a great place to start building your genius emotional value system.

Use your genius mind to build high-vibrating emotions such as joy. Joy has a high energy level; you can tell by the way joy makes you feel. Happiness is another high-vibrating energy. The goal is to place your high-vibrating and genius emotions into action and begin to experience the energy. Begin right away to move into the higher frequency through your emotions and find reasons to express these emotions.

I heard some good advice: be grateful for everything in your life right at this moment. Then begin to make genius changes in your life. It's important to plan your life and learn how to live life by your highest excitements. Planning your life doesn't necessarily mean that every little thing has to be mapped out and written down. The planning I'm going to suggest is mapping out your intentions in your mind with goals written down as guideposts and reminders.

Throughout the entire process of creating your desires, make sure all your thought processes point toward what the spirit wants to experience. This process may be challenging if you are coming out of an unwanted condition. Sometimes it may feel easier to think about the old conditions, but you must stop this thinking immediately. This command I learned from one of Dr. Joe Dispenza's seminars: "Stop. Change. New direction." Your spirit can come through and make such a command and override any current thought processes. After making this command, announce the direction the spirit wants to experience. For example, you're having thoughts about financial troubles and are experiencing the emotion of fear. Stop. Change. New direction! Now, begin to think about a large amount of money coming into your world. It is here that you need to have a plan in place to make large sums of income.

Create a relationship with your higher mind and make it part of your process in creating the things you desire. I am asking you to become aware of this process and remove any negative thoughts and emotions. One of my favorite ways the higher mind communicates is through the imagination. Communication with the higher mind works great if you're a meditator. Before your meditation, set the stage by deciding what you would like to accomplish. You can use your desire affirmations from the workbook to review before going into meditation. Many times, I like to repeat the affirmation to get started, and if I drift off with cluttered thoughts, I repeat the affirmation to create focus.

When the imagination kicks in, it's time to be the observer and pay attention to the details of the images. Don't try to control the image, or it will disappear. Once the images are in the subconscious mind, you can always refer to them. When referring to the images, you can move your feelings into the images. Use your feelings to bring in your genius emotions and feel the excitement and emotions of the event. This activity can spark more communication from the higher mind and bring in more detail.

The Universe in all its magnificence is always working with us; all we have to do is remember!

—Keith Thompson

- **The observer:** I first learned about being the observer in the movie *What the Bleep Do We Know!?* (2004). It is that movie that attracted me to Dr. Joe Dispenza's work.

  To observe who you are and to observe others around you can be a revelation. Watching yourself be yourself is to be aware of your emotions, thoughts, feelings, and actions. When observing others, you are watching their, emotions, thoughts, feeling, and actions in a non-judgmental way. When an emotion does surface, observe that emotion and see where it leads you. These are tools we can use at the spirit level to discover belief systems in the subconscious mind. Ask the question, "What belief do I have that supports this emotion?"

  Observe your environment to see what you're creating in your world. Start by looking at your environment in a nonjudgmental way. Wherever you find yourself, this is your environment. Discover where your emotions are in your environment. The emotions are our filters in the environment. Experiencing your emotions can be likened to wearing filters such as yellow glasses and seeing your whole environment with a yellow tint—the darker the energy, the darker the glasses, the darker the environment. When there's no emotion, we have a clearer picture of our environment. This exercise works well with understanding where those filters are in each of our value systems. All filters are emotions, belief systems, and thought processes. When a filter reveals itself to you, decide to keep it or not. If there are any filters you no longer want, make the command, "I choose to remove this emotion from my beliefs." Making a command like this will start the process of removing that emotion from your value systems. Be sure to use this exercise for all your value systems.

- **The ego mind:** You might wonder how the ego mind came into existence. I happen to think the ego mind has been around a long time in three-dimensional reality. My best guess would be it has existed for hundreds of thousands of years in this solar system. The ego mind could be viewed as symbolic of Lucifer, the fallen angel. He would be in his ego mind to believe he fell from the grace of God. The thought of falling from the grace of God would be an illusion because God is everywhere (omnipresent), so there's no place to fall except to believe in the illusion of falling or failing. It is within the illusions that all ego minds reside.

  We can look at our planet's history and see where many societies have fallen. The fall of Atlantis, the fall of the Roman Empire, and the fall of Babylon suggest the fall of ego mind creation at the collective level. Some would argue that the rise and fall of countries is the natural order of things. The perception may be true, but what belief system changes to create the fall? At the time I am writing *A Journey into Value Systems*, here in the United States, we are experiencing the war between love and hate. We have a leader who operates mostly in his ego mind who is creating love-hate divisions in our country. The collective consciousness of Americans is at a pinnacle point in history. We all have love or hate decisions to make about our nation and our people. We, as people, are experiencing the possible rise or fall of our nation. In our society today, we hear about the abuse of using bombs on other countries, random killings on the homeland, and the negative use of high technology all the time. Hatred is the ego mind at work!

  The reason I am addressing this topic in this manner is to show how big the ego mind system can be. The ego mind at the collective level can bring down a nation and even destroy a planet. If you have an interest in the history of our solar system, do some research on a planet called Maldek. Maldek was a planet between Mars and Jupiter and is now the asteroid belt in our solar system. History has it that this planet was blown up and destroyed through the misuse of energy.

We can see the ego mind operating in the behavior of many of our world leaders today. All wars display elements of the ego mind in beliefs, emotions, and thoughts. The collective level of the ego mind can be extremely destructive. We need to protest any world leader who suggests using any bombs on our beautiful planet.

The ego mind is a well-developed system at the body level, emotional level, and throughout our belief systems. A great place to start investigating unwanted lifestyles is at the emotional level; just look for those ego emotions like greed, fear, and hatred.

Let's look at the ego mind. If the genius mind unites everyone and creates harmony, the ego mind must represent separation and disharmony because of the duality nature of our three-dimensional world. It is the ego mind that keeps us trapped in duality or illusions. We are all a part of All That Is, and this is where we find our genius and oneness with All.

- The ego mind is responsible for creating events out of harmony with All That Is.
- All the ego mind's thoughts, emotions, and beliefs create disharmony.

One of the major themes of the ego mind is to find ways to attack a person's body and mind. This is an attack on our emotional values and beliefs and includes your own body and mind. All hatred that stems from race, color, creed, and natural origin is of the ego mind. Hatred is an emotion that needs to go away. We bear a huge responsibility when our spirits are experiencing hatred. Hatred as part of your value systems is a fast way to establish karmic patterns that will be unforeseen and unpredictable in our environment.

If your life is in disharmony, your belief systems are supporting the ego mind. When disharmonious events are happening, you should move to a genius lifestyle. Disharmony and all the associated emotions are the byproducts of the duality we experience.

The ego can pull creativity apart and create duality or illusions. The ego mind is clever at interfering with the natural creative process. We can create positive and negative experiences. We can tune into the energy of the emotion and determine whether it is the genius mind or the ego mind creating the experience.

Keith Reginald Thompson

CHAPTER 3

EMOTIONS OF THE GENIUS AND THE EGO MINDS

This exercise is all about your emotions. This exercise helps you recognize when you're using your genius mind or ego mind in any given situation. For example, if you're arguing with a friend or family member, and you're in the emotion of anger, you are using your ego mind. Another example is putting yourself down and calling yourself names or making negative like "I'm an idiot." At this time, you're using frustration as an emotion that is the ego mind.

Being happy to be alive is part of the genius mindset. Recognizing reasons to be joyful, excited, and at peace is considered a genius emotion in the journey. Remember that the emotions are the end result of the experience. It is with the genius mind's emotions that you want to build your future while removing all ego mind emotions of the past. This process will continue to assist you in transforming negative ego emotions into positive genius emotions.

This easy exercise will help you determine when you're in your genius mind or the ego mind. Understanding this exercise will help you to make clearer decisions more in alignment with your highest possibilities.

On this journey, we have to learn how to use our minds, and one of the ways to do that effectively is through knowing how to use your emotions.

Instructions:

Use emotional words to describe the duality of the genius mind and the ego mind.

In the left column, write down what you feel are the emotional attributes of the genius mind. In the right column, write down what you feel are the emotional attributes of the ego mind.

The genius mind does not recognize the ego mind's emotions. Because the genius mind is in complete opposition to the ego mind, the genius mind is where the energy of love, peace, and happiness resides.

The ego mind of emotions seeks to do us harm or to do damage in the physical world and our physical body. The examples would be anger, hate, and fear.

"But the fruit of the Spirit is love, joy, peace, patience, kindness, goodness, faithfulness, gentleness, and self-control. Against such things there is no Law" (Galatians 5:22–23 KJV).

Emotions of the Genius Mind and the Ego Mind

The Genius Mind	The Ego Mind
love	hate
peace	anxiety
happiness	stress

Sign and Date: _____

CHAPTER 4

DEFINING YOUR GENIUS VALUE SYSTEMS

This information will provide a perspective to help you understand what each value system is. The questions will stimulate more thoughts and bring in awareness of your journey. There are infinite amounts of ways to interpret each value system. The goal here is to find *your* genius value systems.

What we value in our lives makes up the core of who we are. Whether we are doing it consciously or unconsciously, our life decisions are made up of our core values and beliefs. In the following exercise, we'll begin the processes of defining what our genius core values are.

It is important to understand that every one of us lives life according to what we value. Defining your value systems is a discovery exercise. Our daily activities are filled by what we value most and what we think about the most.

A Journey into Health, Career and Personal Development, Wealth and Financial, Family, Social, Spiritual, Emotional and Mental, and Physical values now begins.

INSTRUCTIONS

1. **What are my ten reasons for labeling a value "genius"?**

   Within each value system, define a minimum of ten reasons a value system is important enough to be labeled genius. You can create an associated affirmation with your reason.

   Example: For financial values, a good genius example is to be financially independent.

   In all your value systems, what is it you want to experience and become?

2. **My mission statements for my values.**

   Defining, planning, and acting on your mission within each value system is an important step to bringing excitement, joy, passion, and happiness in your life. Your mission statement will bring awareness about why things exist in your world. Without developing life missions, you may have no idea why your values exist, and you will have less of a chance of bringing your values to a genius level.

- When defining your mission statements, keep them short, memorable, and inspiring.
- Create inspiring plans that connect to your mission statements and fuel them by exciting emotions.
- Act on your plans! Taking action is where the rubber meets the road, and your action will continue the guidance of your higher mind. You will know you're communicating with your higher mind by experiencing your genius emotions. There will be moments of excitement when this communication is happening.

Example: For Career and Personal Development, your mission statement might be: "I transform unwanted ego conditions into genius lifestyle excitements."

3. **What visions do I see with my imagination?**

Within each value system, write down the visions you see with your imagination. An effective way to accomplish this is to take one of your genius reason statements into meditation and use the statement as an affirmation. Repeating affirmations about desires is a good way to spark the imagination in meditation.

4. **What is my inspiring plan of action?**

Make a list of a few exciting action items you can accomplish to get started. When doing your action plan, take the plan as far as your excitement will take you.

Make big changes in each of the value systems; the action statement must represent growth and change.

Example exercises are for all value systems except for Emotional and Physical values. I will address the changes in these values in the associated section.

HEALTH VALUES

1. **What are my ten reasons for genius health values?**

- To live a long life. I am living a long healthy life.
- To have the energy to do everything I want to accomplish. I am full of energy and vitality.
- To enjoy eating organic foods that are good for me.

2. **My mission statement for health value is:**

- My health mission is to take excellent care of my mind and body so I can experience all the wonderful things life has to offer.

3. **What vision do I see with my imagination about health values?**

   + I see myself practicing yoga on the ocean on a nice sunny day while my dog runs in the background having fun smelling things.
   + I see myself drinking lots of water.

4. **What is my inspiring plan of action for health values?**

   + I am meditating every day to improve my mental and physical awareness.
   + I will hire a nutritionist to learn how to eat balanced meals to improve my heart health.
   + I am going to learn yoga.

HEALTH VALUE SYSTEMS

Ask the questions, "Do I love my body?" and "Do I love my mind?"

The Choice

To love our bodies and minds is to promote health, and to hate our bodies and minds is to promote illness. If the two emotions—love and hate—are cohabitating in the body and mind, the body and mind are indeed at war because the emotions of the body and mind are in opposition. From the subconscious mind, the opposition will express feedback to the conscious mind as confusion.

If we choose to be aware of the condition of our bodies, we will find many body signals and feelings to work with to bring our bodies into a healthier arena. The body's voices start as whispers and become louder until the signals of illness have manifested. The key is to catch the signals at the soft whisper stage and deal with destructive habits, emotions, and belief systems at that time. Making changes can be challenging because some of the behaviors may be caused by addiction.

A rash once developed at the base of my spine. I asked the question, "What is causing the rash at the base of my spine?" Before the rash showed up, I had started drinking Guru and other energy drinks. One day, after I drank my energy drink, I noticed itching along the base of my spine. I knew right away it was caffeine that was causing the rash. I was in denial for a while because I enjoyed the effects I was getting from the energy drinks. Here's something else I noticed—I was heading to the bathroom frequently as a result of the caffeine.

The body and mind don't care what they experience because the body and the subconscious mind are subjective and follow the commands of the conscious mind (objective). The genius mind plays an important role here. Good physical and mental health begin with our mental attitude. The body and mind will merrily go down the paths we've selected consciously or unconsciously. We must choose consciously to live a healthier lifestyle with the mind and the body.

Making choices with the understanding of the genius mind will set up a higher vibration in our bodies and minds and allow us to take charge of the activities that are more in alignment with who we are. Meditation can play an important role in developing a strong mental attitude. By going within your mind, you can easily see what thoughts are at the forefront of your mind. Don't like what you see? You can change negative thoughts by no longer giving them attention; you can replace old ego thoughts with genius thoughts. Removing all the hatred, anger, and negative emotions stored in your mind is an important step to a healthier body.

I want to share an extremely powerful technique with you. When I developed this technique, I was practicing my clinical hypnotherapy work. This technique is called "I love you, Joe." Joe was a neighbor of mine when I was in my teens and twenties. We didn't get along at all. As a matter of fact, the relationship was getting dangerous. I felt the emotions of hate and anger toward him, and he, I am sure, felt the same toward me. I even accused him of breaking into my home and stealing my nice stereo equipment. I had to change my attitude of hatred and anger toward him because it was getting the best of me. Whenever I saw Joe, I would move right to those negative emotions. I was totally in my ego mind. I had to change my emotions and behavior.

I started to say "I love you, Joe" in my mind whenever I thought about him instead of sending hate feelings and emotions. Thinking about Joe in that manner was hard for me in the beginning. My hatred and anger wanted to take over. However, I kept at it. It took twenty-eight days for me to change my feelings and emotions about Joe. The feuding stopped! I moved into a new home and haven't seen him since.

The purpose of this exercise is to change your feelings about someone you're scared of, someone you dislike, or someone who's bullying you. It works great with family members. This technique removes the fear or any ego emotions you may be feeling. You say to yourself, "I love you, …" and insert the person's name. Just watch the negative emotions go away. You will feel better about yourself too!

The Addiction Connection

I've also observed that it is important to understand the addictions related to what we put into our bodies. The one addiction I had since the fifth grade was to sodium. I was caught off guard when I realized that a person could be addicted to salt. It started after school when a bunch of us kids would go to Joe's Grocery Store down the street from the elementary school. We would all purchase sour balls (Chinese salty plums). I didn't realize until about fifteen years ago—some thirty years later—that the five little plums in a package contained about 1500 milligrams of salt. I would eat about five packages of these treats in a day. I was unaware I was putting 7500 milligrams of sodium into my body regularly. I've stopped eating sour balls, but the sodium level had reached addiction in my subconscious mind, and it showed up because I continued to eat other salty foods like potato chips, popcorn, corn chips, pies and cake (lots of sodium there), and, yes, Chinese food with soy sauce.

When I was in my late forties, hypertension started showing up in my body. I was perplexed by the test results because I spent a good portion of my life working out with martial arts and sports. I thought I ate well, but there were other things I needed to work through. I began the process of making changes toward improving my health. For me, this was a challenging path. An uncle of mine had a massive heart attack in his fifties; as a result, fears that I had bottled-up began to surface. Those darn Lipitor television commercials: "And next time you have a heart attack"! One of the questions I like to ask my subconscious and higher mind, for example, is, "Where is hypertension coming from?" Then I realized my mom and dad were on blood pressure medications. I immediately began to understand that I was following family programming about my health and well-being. I decided I was going to choose another path, and I did.

I began to change my viewpoint about health and what I put into my body. I studied health and nutrition. For a while, I became a vegan. I went out and bought a juicing machine and started juicing. Juicing is a great way to put good nutrients into the body. Instead of drinking three or four beers at a sitting with friends, I cut the drinking down to two beers once a week. I am working toward eliminating drinking alcohol altogether. I became a certified professional health coach. I create health affirmations to give me a different focus. For example. "I am now creating a foundation for a healthy heart and lungs." I knew this affirmation meant either getting rid of or cutting back on some habits I enjoyed. I enjoyed socializing with friends, having a few beers. The new affirmations created confusion in my subconscious mind and body because I had a tremendous amount of fear about who I was and how I felt about my body. I had to look at those fears, which had been running in my subconscious mind for a long time. Some of the fears came from my parents' fears; some came from watching unhealthy and violent TV programs. Many of the fears were beliefs about getting old and facing death, and more importantly, I had an unsettled hatred about my body. I realized I placed many judgments on my body and mind. I am sharing this because I know I am not alone in this.

I had to learn to let go of all those fears and stop judging my body and other people's bodies. I had to learn to love being a black American. I grew up where there was a lot of hatred in America against black Americans, Jews, American Indians, Mexicans, and a host of other nationalities and colors. If people looked different, there was a reason to hate them. I grew up thinking this was normal behavior. Hatred isn't normal! Hatred is a mental illness. If there's a major illness in the physical body, the emotion of hatred is the first place to look in mental health. To hate another person or your body for any reason is being an egotist. The United States is a country that prides itself in welcoming everyone into our county. All the people here except the American Indians are from somewhere else! It seems ironic to live in a country where we are the melting pot of the world but we still live with so much hatred because of race and color.

I had to learn to love my body and be a good host to my body. I have learned to say, "I love you, body, and thank you for your service." I am learning to be a good host to my body. It has been challenging. I know these types of practices raise the vibration of the body and mental health.

The process continues!

HEALTH VALUES

1. **What are my ten reasons for genius Health values?**

    • _____

    • _____

    • _____

    • _____

    • _____

    • _____

    • _____

    • _____

    • _____

    • _____

2. **My mission statement for Health values:**

    _____

    _____

    _____

    _____

3. **What vision do I see with my imagination pertaining to Health values?**

    _____

    _____

    _____

    _____

4. **What is my inspiring plan of action for Health values?**

    •   _____

        _____

    •   _____

        _____

    •   _____

        _____

CAREER AND PERSONAL DEVELOPMENT VALUES

The Career and Personal Development value systems ask the questions, "What are my burning desires in life?" and "On what level do I choose to provide my services?"

What are your burning desires? Chances are those desires are your latent talents. One of the beautiful powers of our minds is that all we must do is choose and then become. The key is to trust and allow the genius mind to show you the path. In developing talents, it may take years to become an expert. The journey may be well worth it! I can look back on my life and see the journey I've taken. Way back when I was thirteen years old, I was asked, "Do you want to live as a good person or a bad person?" Choosing to be a good person has given me a lot of powerful tools and insights, many of which are within this book.

From the time I decided to live a good life when I was thirteen years old, I realized that I am working on a guided journey with many options. It took years to develop some of my talents. Most of these talents I discovered in my twenties and never let go of them. These talents led me to a lot of lessons, successes, and balance in my life. Whenever there was a shortcoming, I had many tools to fall back on. My experience history includes therapist, manufacturing consultant, numerical control programmer, tool designer, planner, martial artist, meditator, father, and friend.

The Path

The journey of remembering and learning is part of the excitement of being on the correct career or personal development path. A word of caution: a path that doesn't make you feel good or excited about what you're doing is not the correct career or personal development path. Make another choice! I grew up following a family tradition by working for an aerospace company. My mother was my biggest challenge because she couldn't relate to me as a clinical hypnotherapist specializing in past-life regression. Hypnotherapy didn't fit her Christian belief system.

Many times, we respond to the suggestions of others instead of going into the core of our being. Your feelings will let you know if you're on your genius path. Ask the genius part of you to bring in those talents, and ask your higher mind to make it obvious that it's the correct direction.

The Vision

Having a vision is an important part of understanding how a career or personal development will be applied. For growth, the vision must be greater than the current level at which we find ourselves. In other words, we must serve a higher purpose than ourselves. For example, the child who sweeps the floor and helps clean around the house is serving a higher purpose for the family. The person who goes out and works for a corporation is serving a higher purpose for the city and family. A person who wants to become involved in the city at the government level must at least have a higher vision to serve the state. To become involved at the state level, we need a higher purpose to serve the country, and then from country to world and from the world to the universe. Some may say, "Hey, isn't serving God the highest purpose?" and my answer would be yes, and All That Is operates on all these visions.

Get your imagination involved with your career and personal development. Ask your higher mind what your purpose is for being on Earth during this period. Many people forgot why they are here, and many people don't ask. There are many stories about people who died in their twenties and were buried in their sixties. Do something great; the world will thank you for it!

The Present

One of my biggest challenges on this path and developing my personality was removing fears and past guilts and doubting myself. The more I removed these ego emotions, the clearer the genius visions became. The choices I had to make became clearer. Removing ego emotions is key to developing strong personal development that transfers into your career. Remember, one of the purposes of the ego mind is to keep us thinking in the past and creating falsehoods. Fear (false emotions appearing real), guilt, and doubt are ego emotions that will rob your future potential. Stop projecting with those emotions. What I mean by projecting is creating unwanted and unreliable visions.

Create the path of living in the present moment. What do I mean by this? Get into *your* life! Not a life that is run by others' belief systems. Adopt a life in which your genius mind is operating. Surround the present conditions with all your *strengths* in alignment with the highest reasons you can live. Think of only that! Learn to be the observer and watch for opportunities the Universe provides. Being the observer means removing all judgments about yourself and your environment. Remember—emotions are the filters we see in our environment. When we remove all our emotions in any given situation, we develop clairvoyance, clairaudience, and clairsentience in all our experiences.

In developing the values of career and personal development, ask your genius mind what those values are. Look for a sense of excitement and adventure. Once your idea has been given to you—and it will if you ask—the next step is to ask, "What's my first step to take?" The answer may come in many ways.

CAREER AND PERSONAL DEVELOPMENT VALUES

1. **What are my ten reasons for genius Career and Personal Development values?**

   + _____

   + _____

   + _____

   + _____

   + _____

   + _____

- _____
- _____
- _____
- _____

2. **My mission statement for Career and Personal Development values:**

_____

_____

_____

3. **What vision do I see with my imagination pertaining to Career and Personal Development values!**

_____

_____

_____

_____

4. **What is my inspiring plan of action for Career and Personal Development values action statements?**

- _____

_____

- _____

_____

- _____

_____

EMOTIONAL AND MENTAL VALUE SYSTEMS

The emotional value systems ask the question, "How do I feel about and react to everything in my world?"

"The conscious mind becomes the responsible ruler and guardian of the subconscious mind. It is this high function which can completely reverse conditions in your life" (Haanel 1916, 10).

The Ruler

Emotional values are important when we talk about the child in the subconscious mind. The subconscious mind is subservient to the conscious mind. Also, the subconscious mind is the child not because it lacks anything, but because it is subjective. The child follows the direction of the conscious mind (ruler and guardian) or other people, like parents, who might be in control of an individual. As the individual gets older, the ruler (conscience) can choose to use the genius mind or ego mind emotions during any situation. If you're an adult still and controlled by your parents, I recommend investigating what's going on. The child (subconscious) doesn't question the information coming in if it is not screened by the guardian at the gate. The child will accept everything to be true, whether it is true or not. Many times, we have thoughts and emotions that are not ours. These thoughts and emotions were picked up or handed down from parents or someone else's belief systems. A good example of this involves race. Our different belief systems about our different races in the world have been handed down for many generations. Many race beliefs range from hate to love depending on the personal perspective and where a person lives.

There could be thousands of bits of true and false information running in your subconscious mind right now. Many of these programs are downloads from watching television. According to the Nielsen ratings, the average person watches five hours of television a day. Also, for each hour of network television, there are sixteen minutes of commercial programming. In one week, the average person watches thirty-five hours of television, which means two hours per week of unsolicited commercials! That is 104 hours of commercials a year! Have you ever seen a commercial run multiple times within a few minutes? That is subconscious programming. Be aware of what's going into your mind.

We get information with positive (genius) and negative (ego) viewpoints from friends and family members. We agree with much of the cultural thinking and emotional content because of our childhood age. Many of these old thought processes and much emotional content has a direct relationship with our emotional and mental health. If you have serious health problems, it is extremely important to review what the associated emotions are. From this perspective, it may be the emotions that are causing health problems. Discover who the people are that are related to the emotions, all the mental programming, negative thoughts, and belief systems that may be affecting the illness. In Louise Hay's book, *Heal Your Body*, she gives many examples of body illnesses related to certain mental behaviors and beliefs. For example, "Cancer: Deep hurt. Longstanding resentment. Deep secret or grief is eating away at the self. Carrying hatreds." (Hay 1987, 22). A deep hurt can impact your mental attitude. Emotions associated with deep hurt must be transformed back into genius emotions. Use the "The Emotional Balancing System" to help in the transformation process.

The ruler (conscience) is the one that adds fuel (energy) to the emotions playing out by giving them attention. When attention stops, emotions decrease. It is up to you to use the genius mind to determine the qualities of your emotions. Emotions out of control will produce the same in your environment. An angry person can be consumed by emotions, and there will be unpredictable results in his or her environment. Emotions are a powerful level of your subconscious mind and value systems. The ruler must be under control and not abuse the power of the child.

You Are in Charge

Being aware of feelings is a powerful awakening to who and what we choose to be. Instead of just flying off the handle and having no control over the emotions, to be angry will now be a choice, and feeling love will now be a choice. We can take charge of our emotions and display them in a way that is environmentally friendly. Remember, emotions are the result of experience. If an alcoholic has a bad day, he or she may display the emotion of anger. He goes out and gets drunk. He drives his car and gets in an accident. The accident kills two adults and one child. The emotions of anger may have been the driving engine that led to the accident. The results of his anger turned into a big karmic mess. Now he's left with the consequences of the environment. We hear about these types of incidents all the time. If this person had the emotions of peace and calm, he might not even have had the urge to drink to get drunk. By the way, the conscious mind becomes unconscious when drugs or alcohol is introduced to the body.

We have all the right tools within us. All we must do is learn how to correctly use what we have. If you use your mental and emotional mind for excitement, for joy, love, and happiness, that is what will manifest in your environment.

The Awareness of the Child Within

"Subconscious has programs in it, its not very much of a creative mind. Its creativity is more of a level of creativity of say 5-year old child." (B. Lipton, 2019).

Every moment of your life from childhood to this very moment has been recorded and stored within your subconscious mind. Within the subconscious mind, you can find the inner child and all its emotions. The subconscious mind is the only place you can find the inner child operating. In the environment, you'll witness the results. It's important to heal childhood emotions that are out of harmony with the genius mind. When you ask the question, "How do I feel about and react to everything in my world?" the inner child may pop up through a forgotten memory.

I had an experience when teaching the parent's value systems section this course, *A Journey into Value Systems*. During a meditation session, I was in a deep level of meditation, and an image of a little three-year-old boy popped up. I asked the question, "Why are you showing me this?" I was speaking to my subconscious and higher mind. Then a flood of emotions (subconscious) started to surface. That little three-year-old boy was in total fear. The sounds and emotions all came back to me. His parents were fighting like a mad cat and an angered dog. I went to that little boy and gave him a big hug. I showed him how our life turned out to this point and assured him that he was safe. Even as I write this story, I'm checking in with the little boy, and his emotions are peaceful and calm.

I had inner child work to do. You can find childhood emotions in all your value systems. Some of the emotions will be generated by the ego mind and are not to any fault of your own. I realized my parents had emotional wounds too! These old emotions must be transformed into genius emotions.

The big hitters for me were family, financial, emotional, and physical values. Chances are the inner child is impacted by the ego emotions that are operating in your life today. If you're a meditator and a prayer, your chances of reaching the inner child are excellent. Be sure to ask your subconscious and higher mind good questions. When there's an image from your imagination, ask the question, "Why are you showing me this?" Remember to develop a relationship with your higher mind.

"Unless you change and become like little children, you will never enter the kingdom of heaven" (Matthew 18:3 New International Version).

There's one more thing I would like to mention about the subconscious mind as the child. Have you ever been told by a parent or a sibling that your imagination isn't real? If you have, remove that belief! The imagination is the creative center of the child (subconscious). The imagination comes from higher mind! That is where the child creativity center is. The creative center comes from what we see in our higher mind and becomes our link to the kingdom of heaven.

Genius Mental Attitude

Our emotions and mental attitudes are the driving engines of the things we manifest in life. As you now know, we have our genius (positive) emotions and ego (negative) emotions. The genius emotions of joy, happiness, and excitement will produce their equivalents in the environment. The ego emotions of hatred, meanness, and anger will produce their equivalents and may show up negatively in our environments.

The emotions are the filters we see and experience in life! If you don't like what you're experiencing, change the emotions. That statement is a bold comment to make. One of the things I had to learn was the mental attitude of gratitude from my current life positions and situations. Being in a state of gratitude has a humbling effect on my behavior. For me, humbleness recognizes a higher presence. Realizing this higher presence gives me the determination to accomplish things I desire.

Napoleon Hill, in his book, *Think and Grow Rich*, became known for the attitude known as positive mental attitude (PMA). I'm going to introduce a new acronym: GMA (genius mental attitude). A genius attitude gives you genius internal power. It's an attitude that is practiced repeatedly. Having genius mental attitudes in each of your value systems inspires powerful emotions that create a shield around your genius activities. Focus on your objectives. View focus as a mental attitude. GMA builds a solid mental attitude around your value systems.

One of my personal genius mental attitudes is the warrior mental attitude. I use the warrior mentality when practicing martial arts (physical and health values). I've incorporated the warrior attitude in protecting my family, and sometimes my warrior attitude comes out in the social arena, helping e to stand my ground when I'm challenged. We can easily play the roles of mental attitudes. I want to point out the genius mentality has nothing to do with being weak mentally.

Exercise examples of emotional values:

1. **What is my genius mental attitude for each value system?**

    + Family values: The father, provider
    + Physical values: The observer, gratitude
    + Spiritual values: To unite

2. **What are my genius emotions for each value system?**

Use your genius emotions defined in the Emotions of the Genius and the Ego Mind exercise.

EMOTIONAL AND MENTAL VALUES

1. **What is my genius mental attitudes for each value system?**

    *   Career and Personal values: _____

    *   Emotional values: _____

    *   Family values: _____

    *   Financial values: _____

    *   Health values: _____

    *   Physical values: _____

    *   Social values: _____

    *   Spiritual values: _____

2. **What are my genius emotions for each value system?**

    *   Career and Personal values: _____

    *   Emotional values: _____

    *   Family values: _____

    *   Financial values: _____

    *   Health values: _____

    *   Physical values: _____

    *   Social values: _____

    *   Spiritual values: _____

3. My mission statement for Emotional and Mental values:

    _____

    _____

    _____

4. **What is my inspiring plan of actions for Emotional and Mental values?**

    •   _____

        _____

    •   _____

        _____

    •   _____

        _____

FAMILY VALUE SYSTEMS

The Family Value Systems ask the questions, "Is my relationship with you one of love or of hate?" and "Why do we have this belief system in our family anyway?"

"Your subconscious is the storehouse of memory and within your subconscious are recorded your experiences since childhood" (Murphy 1962, 71).

The Beginning

When we are born on this planet and into a family, that is the beginning of our journeys. The subconscious mind is new, and the recording has begun; it is the environment (physical values) that become the newborn's biggest influence when he or she is awake. Newborns learn how to use their physical senses. The feelings of newborns help them to know their environment, the emotional structure of their families, as well as the physical structure of each family member. Their knowledge increases as they learn how to crawl and then walk and advance to other physical activities. The subconscious mind, from the beginning, runs all the vital body functions and helps newborns grow their bodies in the physical realm. Just look at a baby's growth in one year. The baby learns to walk, speak, and show feelings. The growth of the baby's subconscious mind is at work. The family members are the teachers of the newest member. The baby's thought processes (language), feelings, emotions, and beliefs are learned from the family.

"The most influential perceptual programming of the subconscious mind occurs from birth through age six" (Lipton 2010).

In the family value systems, the parents are responsible for teaching other value systems to members of the family. Speaking in general, parents establish their careers and personal development and pass this information forward.

The emotional values of the parents range from "I love you" to "I hate you" and hundreds of different emotions in between. An example of this is parents who are loving and affectionate one moment and then at each other's throats, yelling and screaming, in the next. During any of these interactions, emotional values and belief systems are attached and come from both parents. The emotions like joy and anger run through the listening family members and are recorded in their subconscious minds as truths. When the parents are arguing with anger emotions, they are in opposition to each other. When parents experience the emotions of love and joy, they are one with each other. Examples of "I love you" and "I hate you" relationships filter into the siblings' relationships as well as the relationships between child and parents. The thing to remember is that the genius emotions unites relationships, and the ego emotions separates relationships.

The interpretation of how the family is to run is the parents' responsibility.

—Keith Thompson

Because I Said So

Do you remember the "why" stage of your life? It usually begins around the age of four and goes well into the teens. When you asked a question about why something must be this way or that way, do you remember your parents saying, "Because I said so"? You may have been told this by an older sister or brother as well. "Because I say so" is a power play over a young child or teen. The parent is saying, "I'm the one establishing the rules (beliefs) here, and you are to abide by them." The subconscious mind remembers the powerplays and becomes subservient to that parent or those older siblings. This method of interaction has established many of our belief systems, and many of these old beliefs are outdated. They set up a pattern that a parent or older sibling is in control, and their rules and beliefs are to be followed and believed. This pattern (programming) can fall into the categories of all the value systems.

With regrd to the Financial and Wealth values, T. Harv Eker talks about having a financial thermostat. My parents had two different perspectives on how they viewed money. My father made good money but had a gambling addiction with the horses, and my mother's values about money centered around family and building a home. Talk about oil and water mixing! I recommend doing the Parent's Values on Financial and Wealth and explore the values of both parents with regard to money. I remember family events from the time I was six months old.

Health values play a big role in family values. In my private practice, I find that most of the weight issues, stress issues, and smoking issues of my clients relate to their families. One client who was excessively overweight was told as a child by her father that she would gain weight just by smelling food. That is a nasty belief system that promotes guilt emotions. Many subconscious programming from parents is associated with food. I was told to eat all the food on my plate. "Don't you know people are starving in Africa?" Many of the stresses come from parents still in control of their adult offspring. If your parents are in control of your life, look at the emotions in which you are participating and start the process of eliminating unwanted emotions. There are many exercises in this book to assist you.

The "Why do we have this belief anyway?" starts with the family. Different activities start to take place like going to church, Little League activities, watching television, playing family games, and emotional attitudes with family members.

If the parents have lost their spiritual way, you'll see in their children more use of drugs, alcohol, pills; more abuse of their physical bodies; and maybe abuse of family members. The emotional levels here are deep and ego driven. A lot of healing and loving energy needs to take place to remove ego emotions.

If you have experienced serious family dynamics, use The Emotional Balancing Systems to begin the healing process. It's a starting process to see things from the genius side. Also, learn to be the observer and recognize all the emotions displayed around you. Begin to disassociate with the ego emotions. We have to begin the process of breaking through the veil. Remember, emotions are the result of the experience. The emotions and beliefs are connected and relayed back into the environment.

FAMILY VALUES

1. **What are my ten reasons for genius Family values?**

   * _____

   * _____

   * _____

   * _____

   * _____

+ _____

+ _____

+ _____

+ _____

+ _____

2. **My mission statement for Family values:**

_____

_____

_____

_____

3. **What vision do I see with my imagination pertaining to Family values!**

+ _____

+ _____

+ _____

+ _____

+ _____

4. **What is my inspiring plan of actions for family values?**

+ _____

_____

+ _____

_____

+ _____

_____

UNDERSTANDING YOUR PARENTS' VALUES

What makes or made your parents tick? Whatever it is could be what is making you tick. Many of our subconscious programmings are hand me downs. In other words, they are belief systems we did not select; rather, they were part of the family dynamics.

This discovery exercise will help you discover your parent's value systems from your current perspective. Pick an important period in your life during which your parents were a big influence on you, positively or negatively. At about the age of four, the conscious mind starts its development. The "why" stage begins during this period. If one or both parents were missing during your upbringing, pick one or two people who had a big influence in your life. This exercise will help trigger where some of your values began.

1. **List your parents' value systems during the period you've selected from the most important value to the least important value.**
2. **What were the key points about your parents' beliefs?**

To answer this question, find key points about how your parents related to you and their world. What were the values your parents were instilling in you? Take notes if the value system needs updating to a new belief system. There are eight sections to use in your evaluation.

1. **What is my approximate age at the time of this evaluation?**

_____

Value Systems: Career and Personal Development, Emotional and Mental, Family, Financial and Wealth, Health, Physical, Social, Spiritual

My _____ **Value System (Parent) Date:**

1.	
2.	
3.	
4.	
5.	
6.	
7.	
8.	

My _____ Value System (parent) Date:

1.	
2.	
3.	
4.	
5.	
6.	
7.	
8.	

2. _____ (father, mother, grandparents, adoptive parent).

What are the key points about my parent's belief about _____ value?

+ _____

_____

_____

+ _____

_____

_____

+ _____

_____

_____

_____ (Parent)

What are the key points about my parent's belief about _____ value?

+ _____

_____

_____

♦ _____

_____

_____

♦ _____

_____

_____

_____ (Parent)

What are the key points about my parent's belief about _____value?

♦ _____

_____

_____

♦ _____

_____

_____

♦ _____

_____

_____

_____ (Parents)

What are the key points about my parent's belief about _____value?

♦ _____

_____

_____

+ _____

  _____

  _____

+ _____

  _____

  _____

_____ (Parent)

What are the key points about my parent's belief about _____ value?

+ _____

  _____

  _____

+ _____

  _____

  _____

+ _____

  _____

  _____

_____ (Parent)

What are the key points about my parent's belief about _____ value?

+ _____

  _____

  _____

+ _____

_____

_____

+ _____

_____

_____

_____ (Parent)

What are the key points about my parent's belief about _____value?

+ _____

_____

+ _____

_____

+ _____

_____

_____

What are the key points about my parent's belief about _____value?

+ _____

_____

+ _____

_____

＊

FINANCIAL AND WEALTH VALUE SYSTEMS

If you were to develop a genius Financial and Wealth value system, what would it look like? What would you have in place to assure financial and wealth abundance? Would your Financial and Wealth values improve your health and social values? Would your Financial and Wealth values bring you closer to your physical and spiritual values? All these questions I have pondered. Here are some ideas I would like to share with you.

I've been fortunate enough to have met some very interesting millionaires and studied many of their programs. During the years 2002 through 2008, I studied lots of millionaires' concepts. I joined a program called The Enlightened Millionaire Institute (EMI). This program was developed by Robert G. Allen and Mark Victor Hansen. The Enlightened Millionaire Institute helped people become millionaires through real estate, writing books, marketing, and adopting information from successful millionaires. I first chose real estate as my focus and did well. I have to say, I was looking good financially on paper. I ended up owning three homes before I got out of the real estate business. Fixing and repairing homes was a lot of work for me. I attempted to do a lot of the work myself. Some of the jobs were beyond my skillset, and I had to hire professionals. I did not know enough about fixing and repairing homes to be in that business.

Robert Allen is a big real estate giant and is well known for addressing multiple streams of income (MSI). MSI means incorporating many streams of income into your financial structure.

Mark Victor Hansen is the founder and co-author of the Chicken Soup for the Soul series of books. He taught many of the seminars about learning how to become an author. He believes that there's a book in each of us.

I heard about Dr. John Demartini through a live interview with EMI. What fascinated me about Dr. John was that he lived on a ship called *The World* that traveled around the world. I thought that was so cool! I started studying Dr. John Demartini's work. I did the Demartini Breakthrough Experience. Amazing! I learned about people's dynamics and how I viewed people in his program. I studied many of his wealth programs; he has a strong background in understanding value systems. In one of Dr. John's programs, he talked about carrying around in his pocket the amount of money he wanted to make in a day. I found this curious. I was in Houston doing one of Dr. John's seminars, and I asked him about carrying his daily income in his pocket. He said he made way too much money at that time! He showed me his wallet. It contained about half an inch's worth of thick, crisp, new hundred-dollar bills. I didn't ask him how much he had. But Dr. John had shifted my thinking. This man can purchase anything he wants at any time he wants. That's power and abundance.

Another millionaire I met was T. Harv Eker. He introduced a genius program called The Millionaire Mind. He designed this three-day seminar to help his audience recondition their minds to think like millionaires. He had participants go through all their beliefs about money. An example might be, "Money doesn't grow on trees!" Participants then split up into groups and had discussions about their outdated beliefs about money. Throughout the entire seminar, participants were encouraged to repeat the affirmation "I have a millionaire mind!" We went through confession about any guilts we had about money. One of my sons confessed that he had taken money from my coin sock. I kept all my excess change in a sock. Sometimes it contained two to three hundred dollars! I knew someone had taken money, but I didn't know which family member it was. Come to find out it was everyone's go-to funding place!

The emotional exercise always brought out the tears in people. After the emotional exercise, Mr. Eker would send us through emotional healing to remove those unwanted emotions.

If you have any emotional healing to do about money issues, use The Emotional Balancing Systems.

I went to five Millionaire Mind seminars, all live events. I took my sons to some of the programs and went with friends to others. Looking back, I believe this was a powerful program. Millionaire Mind seminars taught me to become aware of my Financial and Wealth belief systems. The Financial and Wealth values have been challenging for me. My biggest lessons have been in this value system.

During the period when I was studying the millionaire concepts, the movie *The Secret* was released. I met many of the experts in the movie. *The Secret* presented a tremendous amount of information. I felt that some of the information was misleading because it made me feel I could heal my body and be a millionaire the next day. Nice vision! One of the things *The Secret* never emphasized was the years each expert had in studying the secret. Many of the experts had studied for more than twenty years. My point for bringing up the years of experience is to address the fact that it takes time to incorporate this information into your belief system. Stuart Wilde, in his video, *The Complete Guide Book to the Law of Attraction*, states that "ten years of a life of a human being development is not a long time" (Wilde 2014).

I had to allow myself to grow. I'm still growing to know the universal law of attraction and the universal law of abundance. Remember, the laws are universal laws. Please do not pass the universal laws off as a New Age concept.

"The Law of Attraction is the ability to attract into our lives whatever we are focusing on. It is the Law of Attraction which uses the power of the mind to translate whatever is in our thoughts and materialize them into reality" (thelawofattraction.com 2019).

"The Law of Abundance. Financial Success. There is ample money for everyone who knows how to acquire it and keep it. We live in an abundant universe in which there is sufficient money for all who want it and are willing to obey the laws governing its acquisition. You Can Have All You Want" (Tracy 2019).

One of my favorite books about finance and wealth is *The Science of Getting Rich: How to make money and get the life you want* by Wallace D. Wattles.

"It is easy to understand that the nearer we live to the source of wealth, the more wealth we shall receive" (Wattles 1910, 38).

"Become aware of and recognize fully the fact that the Principle of Power within you is God Himself. You must consciously identify yourself with the Highest" (Wattles 1910).

One of the things I love about this quote is that it recognizes the god within us. Abundance brings us closer to God Himself. Because abundance is a universal law, we can have an abundance of lack if we're thinking that way and still be close to God. Why would that be a choice? People who believe that money is the root of all evil may choose the path of lack. What we think regarding money is what we become.

The principle of power is within us. What if we shifted our thoughts from what the ego wants to what the spirit wants? We would use the genius mind to communicate with the spirit part of us. Then we would move from thought to bringing in the imagination and acknowledging God's principle throughout the entire process. Then we would incorporate the power of gratitude. We incorporate the power of gratitude not because God has an ego. We use the power of gratitude to keep from using *our* ego. We are part of the God process, which includes the universal laws of attraction and abundance if we choose to participate.

"There is a thinking stuff from which all things are made, and which, in its original state, permeates, penetrates, and fills the interspace of the universe" (Wattles 1910, 18).

What we think ultimately comes into our reality. Our original thought and the state of mind we were in when we had it can permeate, penetrate, and fill the interspace of the universe. Would we have a negative thought about money if we knew this? The fact that our thoughts fill the interspace of the universe tells me that this is part of the creation process to abundance. We have the responsibility to think and create images by our thoughts, and the interspace of the Universe is to manifest our creations associated with our thoughts.

> You will never do great things in the external world until you think great things in the internal world.
>
> —Keith Thompson

This quote points right to the level of mind you should use in the creative processes. Without any doubt, you should use your genius mind to reach your highest potential. It's important to decide what the spirit wants to experience because the spirit is beyond the external world. When spirit uses the genius mind, all the emotions, the imagination, and the universal laws become harmonized. You'll know if you're in the internal world when your imagination is involved and the emotions you're feeling bring you joy. It is the ego mind that creates disharmony and negative feelings about money. Leave the ego out of all creative processes to obtain wealth.

Three common traits of the millionaires I met:

1. There was no separation between their careers and their passions. Every millionaire I met had a strong passion for what he or she was doing. There was a focus associated with passion. They were the most focused people in the room. They could draw people into their discussions and engage listeners.
2. They recognized that everyone is a genius. In many of the classes I attended, we would go through the announcement of awakening our genius. Everyone would announce, "I have a genius mind, and I applied my wisdom."
3. They were great marketers. One of the things I was able to do by attending the millionaire classes was to see how each millionaire marketed his or her products. I saw whose products were flying off the shelves and whose products were not. The millionaires who knew their information and had passion about what they were doing did well. Some millionaires abused their marketing power by going straight for the money and charging more than what the product was worth.

FINANCIAL AND WEALTH VALUES

1. **What are my ten reasons for genius Financial values?**

   + _____

   + _____

   + _____

   + _____

- _____
- _____
- _____
- _____
- _____
- _____

2. **My mission statement for Financial values:**

_____

_____

_____

3. **What vision do I see with my imagination pertaining to Financial values!**

- _____
- _____
- _____
- _____
- _____

4. **What is my inspiring plan of action for Financial values?**

- _____

_____

- _____

_____

- _____

_____

THE VALUE OF MONEY

The way we spend our money is directly related to what we value most about our material world.

The Value of Money is a discovery exercise about what we value about money within our financial structure. It is important to understand that every one of us makes, spends, and saves our money according to our eight major value systems and belief systems. What we value most we spend our money on. A mother may go out and spend three hundred dollars for her children's clothing, and the father may go out and spend a thousand dollars on golf clubs. Each family member has a different perspective on how she or he spends money. The mother's values, at that time, centered on Family, and the father's money values centered around Health or Social values.

It is important to note where our Financial and Wealth values are within our eight value system structures at any given time. It is also important to understand what our belief systems are when it comes to money. The awareness of these two important factors is key to where we place our money (win or lose) and how we turn money into material things.

1. **Write a brief summary of your current Financial and Wealth situation:** The question to ask is, "Am I happy with my current Financial and Wealth situation?" If you are not, what needs to change?

2. **What emotions are involved in your Financial and Wealth values?** It has been my observation that emotions and money have a direct link to each other. It is important to note what beliefs and emotions are playing within your financial value systems.

3. **What are your beliefs about money?** Explore the history of your family's financial belief systems. Go back a couple of generations and review your parents' and grandparents' financial belief systems. What are your parents' stories about financial defeats and successes? What belief systems are controlling your current financial situation?

   Example: As a child, my parents taught me that money doesn't grow on trees. I wonder if this belief has had an impact on my buying power or the ability to have the things I wanted.

4. List all your value systems that need financial support. **Become aware of all your value systems that require financial support.**

Income tracking exercise: Track all cash flow coming into your orbit for thirty days. Tracking cash flow will help you see the moods, beliefs, and values of spending money. When money is a present to you, how do you receive it? Do you express gratitude for the income, or do you greeting the income as not enough?

Expense tracking exercise: During an average day, most of us are investing, working for money, spending money, or borrowing money. When we spend money, there associated are value systems, belief systems, and emotions. During this exercise, become aware of your thoughts, emotions, and beliefs to see what surfaces in your mind. There are many ways to process this exercise.

For example: Let say you have a credit card debt, and you feel you may never get the card paid off. Then you're reminded that there's another bill that needs paying and you don't have the money to pay. The emotions of fear set in, and you begin to wonder how all the financial debt will get paid. Now, if you're using affirmations like "I can't afford it," that is your belief system. Of course, this belief must change.

Track all cash flow for thirty days. Tracking cash flow will help you see the moods, beliefs, and your values with regard to spending money. Be sure to include credit card expenses and any bills to be paid.

Saving tracking exercise: Track all cash flow going into savings. Do you have a specific account for saving? Do you have saving accounts for a car or a vacation trip? Are you saving for retirement?

Note: If you are married or in a serious relationship, be sure your significant other does the exercises. The outcome could be revealing!

1. **Write a brief summary of your current Financial and Wealth situation:**

_____

_____

_____

_____

_____

_____

_____

_____

_____

_____

_____

2. **What emotions are involved with my Financial and Wealth values?**

    • _____

    • _____

    • _____

    • _____

    • _____

3. **What are my beliefs about money?**

    • _____
       _____
       _____

    • _____
       _____
       _____

    • _____
       _____
       _____

    • _____
       _____
       _____

    • _____
       _____
       _____

    • _____

• _____

_____

_____

_____

• _____

_____

_____

4. **List all your value systems that needs financial support:** Career and Personal development, Emotional and Mental, Family, Health, Physical, Social, Spiritual.

• _____

• _____

• _____

• _____

• _____

• _____

Receiving Income Tracking Example:

Monthly

Income	Career	Emotional	Family	Financial	Health	Physical	Social	Spiritual
Microsoft	$7,600							
401K				$335.00				
Fitness Trainer					$500.00			
Stocks and Bonds				$750.00				
Total	**$7,600**			**$1085.00**	**$500.00**			
$9,185.00								

In this example, there are four multiple streams of income: two passive incomes and two labor incomes. Passive income makes money that is not from an employer or labor work. The 401K and stocks and bonds are passive income.

The income from being a fitness trainer is listed under health values because it is the highest value for doing the job. The trainer is doing her job because she wants to improve the health of other people.

Be sure to track your income-to-expense ratio. Take note on how your financial blueprint looks.

Expense Tracking Example:

Monthly

Expenses	Career	Emotional	Family	Financial	Health	Physical	Social	Spiritual
Grocery shopping			$220.50					
Mortgage						$1875.00		
Education	$125.00							
Night out							$98.00	
Church								$120.00
Juice Bar					$10.95			
Car Note						$630.00		
Clothes			$325.00					
Dinner							$53.00	
Alcohol		$28.75 (-)						
Credit Payment				$72.00				
Total	$125	$28.75	$545.50	$72.00	$10.95	$2,505	$151.00	$120.00

My value system, according to my expenses:

1. Physical
2. Family
3. Social
4. Career and Personal Development
5. Spiritual
6. Financial and Wealth
7. Emotional
8. Health

Note: There are many ways to interpret your values when it comes to spending money. For example, there are several categories that work with grocery shopping. If you are buying food for your family, groceries can easily fall under Family values. If you're into health and fitness and living alone, groceries can fall under Health values. Or, feel free to split the cost under different value systems. The same goes for a mortgage. I have it listed under Physical values. For me, Physical value involves my environment. For some journeyers, the mortgage may fall under Family values or even Financial values if the home is an investment.

If you're improving your life and reconstructing your financial situation, there may be some expenses that are negative expenditures. For example, buying cigarettes could be a negative expense.

Place a negative symbol next to the amount (-) that will let you know this behavior is to change. The following exercise, Things I Desire, is a great place to address values you no longer want.

One more thing I'd like mention about spending money—be sure to pay close attention to your emotions and self-talk during exchanges. People who are supported by the abundance of lack will experience the emotions of fear, and thoughts of "I am broke, and I never have money!" To make changes in Financial and Wealth, you must stop these kinds of emotions. Deciding to have financial wealth is a worthy goal. Use the material in *A Journey into Value Systems* to assist you. If you need a new career or more personal development, use the Career and Personal Development value chapter to assist you. The Emotional and Mental Value chapter is another great chapter to assist you in your finances.

Simple Savings Example:

				Monthly				
Savings	**Career**	**Emotional**	**Family**	**Financial**	**Health**	**Physical**	**Social**	**Spiritual**
Vacation			$125.00					
Savings Account				$400.00				
Son's Education	$100.00							
Investments				$750.00				
New Car						$300.00		
Wife's Birthday							$50.00	
Total	**$100**	**$0**	**$125.00**	**$1150.00**	**$0**	**$300.00**	**$50.00**	**$0**

My value system, according to my savings:

1. Financial and Wealth
2. Physical
3. Family
4. Career and Personal Development
5. Social
6. Emotions
7. Health
8. Spiritual

Note: One of the things T. Harv Eker stressed in his Millionaire Mind seminars is that we should have multiple savings accounts to support our values, and we should use each account strictly for the assigned purpose.

Receiving Income Tracking:

Monthly

Income	Career	Emotional	Family	Financial	Health	Physical	Social	Spiritual
Total								

Expense Tracking

Month/Week/Day _____

Expenses	Career	Emotional	Family	Financial	Health	Physical	Social	Spiritual
Value Totals								

Total Expenses:

Savings Tracking

Month/Week/Day _____

Savings	Career	Emotional	Family	Financial	Health	Physical	Social	Spiritual
Value Totals								

Total Expenses:

My Financial Values according to expenses and savings

Value System from Expenses	Value System from Savings
1.	
2.	
3.	
4.	
5.	
6.	
7.	
8.	

PHYSICAL VALUE SYSTEMS

The physical value system asks the question, "What do I choose to see and experience in my world?"

We are in physical bodies on a physical planet and are having physical experiences. From the perspective of the journey into value systems, physical values represent what we choose to see and experience on Earth in our physical bodies. There are two major categories of our physical experiences on Earth. One: what we experience as collective human experiences. Two: what you and I see and experience individually. In other words, what we are creating in our physical realities.

The Collective Experiences

The first tier of collective experiences are beliefs from the world perspective. For example, what is needed to keep the body functioning? A certain amount of water to drink or food to eat, air to breathe, and obeying the laws of gravity are collective agreements for living on this planet. Human reproduction could be part of a collective agreement.

The second tier of collective agreements and experiences is what to believe. What to believe comes from families, school systems, religious structures, political, and government structures.

The third tier of collective agreements are the social groups that have similar belief systems to yours. Television could be considered collective agreements in the popularity of show and downloads to the subconscious mind from commercials to buy things. If you are among those who watch, on average, five and a half hours of television (tell-a-vision) per day, chances are high that television programming is shaping a lot of your beliefs, and those beliefs become experiences. If you're a big television watcher, I am encouraging you to look at the visions of television you are attracting. There is violence everywhere on television. Do you see how it's playing out on our planet? News, especially local news, is based on triggering emotions. Next time you watch a local news program, do a feeling check on your emotions and see how close you are to feeling excited. If you're experiencing anxiety and depression, review your past week or month of television watching and decide if you're watching too much news or violent television programs.

The Individual Experiences

The individual experiences are what I call the "I am" experiences. I am experiences are your own unique experiences in the world, good or bad. When being aware of these experiences, we move into what our spirit wants to experience instead of only following others' collective agreements. What we physically see and experience reflects our values. Our physical values encompass all the other value systems and play them back in our physical reality. Our physical experience is the mirror of the "I am." All your rewards and challenges are right here in what you are experiencing in the physical world. Making definite choices of what you want to experience in physical reality becomes important.

Keep in mind, if you're having health challenges, the activities contributing to your health are played out in your physical reality. A good example is having issues with your lungs while, in your physical reality, you smoke two packs of cigarettes a day. The problem is in plain sight. However, when you realize smoking is a physical value, and it has a direct negative effect on your health, this awareness changes things. Well, it should if you want to incorporate a genius lifestyle in health.

The genius mind and the ego mind play very well in physical reality, and it's all governed by the choices we make and what we believe. If you make the decision that the ego mind is at play with cigarette smoking, you can now look at the ego emotions that are triggering the smoking and begin the process of removing its reality.

Living your life by your highest excitement should reside here in the physical experiences. Physical realities are your checkpoints that you're living your life according to your values. Build your genius pathway to build excitement in each of your value systems. For example, I am experiencing financial success in my physical reality.

It becomes important when we say "I" because our subconscious tape recorders turn on and start the communication with the imagination and the universe. It is a big deal if we say, "I am having a bad day" because whatever's happening *is* our physical experience. I am suggesting that this has been created by past thinking or beliefs to set up the emotional filters of having a bad day. When this happens with me, I go right into the element of being the observer and recognize the origin of this event and review the emotions and beliefs. I also look at what value system is involved. Let's say the bad day evolved around Financial values. In the past, I would let the ego emotions dictate future outcomes. Now I review my genius reasons for Financial values and make sure I am working on my mission statement. The review may involve other value systems like Career and Personal Development. I look at my genius reasons for Career and Personal Development and review the mission statement as well.

How You Choose to Appear with Your Body

If you fill your body with love and white light, it will show, and some people will notice. It's simple. Say, "I fill my body with love and white light." The next step is to feel the love and white light coming into your body. Don't be too concerned how the love and light are coming in. You can bathe in it. You can send this energy to a loved one, to the planet, or even to a negative situation to begin the process of changing the outcome. The more you get into this practice, the more you get out of it. This technique is great to use when waking up from sleep and before going to sleep.

Anytime there's a challenge in your physical reality, instead of having a pity party and possibly using drugs and alcohol, use the love and white light technique to move through the issue. The ego mind has no chance to express itself when love and white light are around. Yes, I am asking you to see the light in your physical experiences. I've taken the time to play with the love and light energy a lot. It's wonderful! The most effective way for me is to lie down, close my eyes, allow the love and light to come into the body, and use my genius to determine how this energy is to travel and be used. You can use this energy to direct and guide yourself in each of your value systems.

Awakening the Dreamer

When we lie down to sleep, we dream. During sleep, the higher mind and spirit communicate, and sometimes the spirit brings information back to the subconscious mind. When we dream, we are the dreamer. Dreaming is something we naturally do. It's who we are.

Become the dreamer in the physical world when you're awake in the physical body. The technique is to reverse the process and move into dreamland while you are awake in the physical world. The dream exercise is fun and inspires curiosity. See yourself dreaming at any given time throughout the day. Be curious and ask questions about the events you see or people you see. Ask questions like, "Who are you?" or "What is this event about?" Look for symbols and signs of your goals and desires. Be aware of how things are constantly changing. Watch how people are there and then suddenly gone.

If you've made your desire lists in *A Journey into Value System: Cracking the Genius Code*, practice bringing your desires into the physical world real-time through the dreamlike state. Know that your spirit is involved in these events and can influence them at any time. Have fun!

PHYSICAL VALUES

1. **List one high-excitement idea you want to experience in each of the value systems**

   + Health values

     _____

     _____

   + Career and Personal development values

     _____

     _____

   + Emotional and Mental attitude values

     _____

     _____

   + Family values

     _____

     _____

   + Financial values

     _____

     _____

   + Social values

     _____

     _____

+ Spiritual values

_____

_____

+ Physical values

_____

_____

2. **My mission statement for physical value:**

_____

_____

_____

_____

3. **What are my "genius" physical values action statements?**

+ _____

_____

SOCIAL VALUE SYSTEMS

The Social Value System asks the question, "What do I see in you?"

Family influences play a big role in our social networking, and they start in childhood. The social networking starts in the family (values) and move into the neighborhoods and on to education systems, corporations, cities, countries and politics, and the world. All those involved in this social networking brings in their beliefs, their emotions, their feelings, and their thoughts. We interact with people who represent something in our value systems, and we are influenced by their beliefs, as ours influence them. Today, with cell phones and the internet, we can connect to people around the world. With modern transport systems, we can be anywhere in the world within a day or two. We are in an era of networking.

Knowing the teachings in *A Journey into Value System: Cracking the Genius Code* will give you some advantages. You will be able to tell which value systems people are engaged in during conversations or as they are speaking. You will know whether they operate from the genius or the ego mind. When there's a crowd, and you want to learn about the group, you can become the observer to review feelings, emotions, and beliefs about the environment.

> Mirror, mirror, on the wall, what I see in you sticks to me after all!
>
> —Keith Thompson

When we meet someone or pass by another soul on the street, we send off signals of feelings and emotions based on our beliefs. Many times, we choose the energy we want to see or feel in someone who has just crossed our path. The feelings can range from hate or fear to love and a smile. When I was studying the book A Course in Miracles in the early 1980s, the book brought my attention to how much I feared people because of my ego mind. I feared total strangers I had never met before. They would feel the fear I was sending out, and on many occasions, they would send the fear back to me. What a way to interact, right?

I have since learned how to greet strangers even if we don't speak. It ranges from being the observer to sending a smile. My attitude in meeting people has a lot to do with how I want to feel throughout the day. However, if something doesn't feel right, I immediately switch to observer mode.

> Everyone has the power to love or hate.
>
> —Keith Thompson

When you are speaking to someone, what's your message? It is in your speech that you will find your values, emotions, and beliefs. When someone speaks to you, how does it make you feel? What are their emotions saying to you?

The genius and ego minds operate within our social networking systems. When we define our genius value systems and put them to action, we create a network alignment to our desires. We can then attract the desired learning path, and we attract the network alignment that will propel us forward. Social networking and genius values were the path to developing *A Journey into Value Systems*.

We are very much alike and yet so different!

Social Values

1. **What are my genius social connections for each value system?** Connections can be social groups for career and personal development or social groups for health and well-being.

  - Career and Personal development values: _____

    _____

  - Emotional and Mental values: _____

    _____

  - Family values: _____

    _____

  - Financial values: _____

    _____

  - Health values: _____

    _____

  - Physical values: _____

    _____

  - Social values: _____

    _____

  - Spiritual values: _____

    _____

2. **My mission statement for Social values:**

    _____

    _____

    _____

    _____

3. **What is my inspiring plan of action for Social values action statements?**

    * _____

    _____

    * _____

    _____

    * _____

    _____

Spiritual Value Systems

Sometimes the meaning is in the word itself: Spirit-u-all!

The Spiritual Values ask the question, "What do I want my spirit to experience?"

Here's a point of view: We are all geniuses born into a world (Earth) of dualities—light and dark energies! When we are going through the birth process, our physical minds (conscious/subconscious) are wiped clean to create a new experience for the soul. At birth, the spirit and the body are one. It is the spirit that has all the elements of a genius. When we were born with new physical minds and bodies, we learned to follow the collective agreements first. In doing so, we as individuals risked the chance of losing our individuality and only following a sleeping group. I would define the collective sleeping group as people who search only outside of themselves for answers and who are not aware of their spirit.

Many people on Earth lose sight and communication with their spirit because they follow a collective sleeping group. Unaware people do not realize there's a spirit experiencing the choices. They have the gift of the spirit, but they're asleep to it. The unaware persons forget they're from the spirit world experiencing a physical reality.

Establishing communication with your genius spirit brings in a higher awareness and energy. When people set goals and they have that burning desire to accomplish them, that's spirit. They are no longer operating at the physical level with just the conscious/subconscious mind.

Our genius spirit has been there with us all the time since birth. We were born with our spirit, and we will leave Earth with it. Being aware of your genius spirit and operating your physical body through spirit and placing your genius mark on our planet is the awakening! There are challenges and rewards from this point of view.

Our genius has been awakened when we realize we are spirits having physical experiences through our physical bodies. The genius part of us knows we can create our reality and experience the gifts and wonders of the physical world.

The statement "You are greater than you think you are" points to our spirit.

Spiritual Values

1. **What are my ten reasons for genius Spiritual values?**

    + _____

    + _____

    + _____

    + _____

    + _____

    + _____

+ _____

+ _____

+ _____

+ _____

2. **My mission statement for Spiritual values:**

_____

_____

_____

_____

3. **What vision do I see with my imagination pertaining to Spiritual values?**

+ _____

+ _____

+ _____

+ _____

+ _____

4. **What is my inspiring plan of action for Spiritual values action statements?**

+ _____

_____

+ _____

_____

+ _____

_____

Sign and Date: _____

CHAPTER 5

THE VALUE OF TIME

"Until you value yourself, you won't value your time. Until you value your time, you will not do anything with it" (Peck 1978).

Let's say you suddenly find yourself transported to a different city in a different state three thousand miles away from home and you have no directions for getting back. You don't know how you got to this place, but you're here, and you need to find your way back home. Your mission is to find your way back home in an exciting way. How would you do it? The first task is to know where you are.

The purpose of the value of time exercise is to discover where you are in your values about time. If you want to put value in your life, the way you spend your time becomes important; it has a direct relationship to what you value most. Time is your opportunity to live life at your highest excitements.

Health, Career and Personal Development, Wealth and Financial, Family, Social, Spiritual, Emotional and Mental, and Physical

Instructions:

For the best impact of the time study, work it in order. If you are married or in a serious relationship, be sure to have your significant other do the exercises.

1. **List your value system according to importance from the highest to the least**

   Write down the eight value systems listed above in order from the most important to the least important according to where you think they are currently in your life.

2. **a) My weekday and weekend activities**

   List eight or more things you do that take up the bulk of your time during an average day. For example, most people have an eight-hour-a-day job, spend time with family members and friends, and sleep at night.

   Be honest with yourself here. According to the Nielson ratings, the average American watches almost five and a half hours of tell-a-vision a day. Be sure to include sleep time in your daily activities. Do your best to get as close to 168 hours in the one week as you can. It's okay to use "miscellaneous" to fill up the "I don't know where the time went" space. You can do a time study for one week to get a more accurate assessment of your value of time.

b) List the approximate hours next to the daily activities.

The daily activities can fall under several different value systems. You can split the activities into different value system groups if you want to. For example, sleep can fall under an Emotional and Mental value for the mind, Physical value for the body, and Spiritual value for the spirit.

c) Match the appropriate value system next to the weekday/weekend activities.

From the list of weekday and weekend activities, match each activity with the appropriate value system. If multiple value systems are associated with the activity, use the Connected Value System column.

d) Connecting the value system

Adding a connecting value system gives you a deeper understanding of what's going on within that activity.

e) Checkmark the activities that need to change. With your writing tool, put an "x" next to the activities that should be replaced with something new and exciting. Note that you now have five hours to convert into different energy by eliminating television.

e) Check	a) Weekday Activities	b) Hours	c) Value System	d) Connected Value System
	Working at Barnes and Noble	6.5	Financial	
x	Watching television	5.0	Emotional	Physical
	College courses	4.0	Personal develop.	Career

3. **Total up the number of hours for the week.**

Now, add up the total hours in each value system for weekday and weekend.

4. **Compare daily value systems**

Write in your important value system structure from the first exercise. In the Daily Activity Value System column, write the value system with the highest accumulated hours to the least. Now compare the two columns.

5. **My exciting new weekday and weekend activities**

Without judging yourself, decide what you would love to experience in the eight values. If everything were possible for you, how would your day look? Now make a list of your exciting daily activities. Be sure to include hours and the value system.

6. **My value system from an exciting point of view**

    If necessary, create a new value system order that reflects your new and exciting direction.

7. **a) My exciting direction**

    From your exciting weekday and weekend activity list, pick out the important and exciting activities you want to incorporate into your life. I recommend highlighting the exciting activities so they will stand out in your genius mind as being important.

    Note: There are a few ways to approach My Exciting Direction. The approach I like is to work on one value system at a time and work on some activities within that particular value system. The important piece of this exercise is to get the ball rolling. Allow this exciting activity to become an important part of your life by incorporating it into your daily activities.

    If you're a beginner at goal setting and making life changes, start with changes that will be simple and easy for you. You can pick something like reading books that could start a new interest or career path.

    b) My vision

    Review your new exciting activity, close your eyes, and allow your imagination to entertain all the possibilities of this new direction. It may help to have a partner to engage with during this process. Allow your partner to ask you important questions about this exciting direction. Write down what you see in your imagination.

    This process will help you engage with the genius mind. The genius mind has a direct link to the higher levels of the imagination. Be sure to keep all the images beautiful, prosperous, and exciting.

    c) My intention

    Write down an intention. The intention could be the first step in your exciting new activity. An intention is a form of acting with a focus and a purpose. The actions that you take will greatly impact your exciting new direction. An example would be going to your attorney's office to get your license for a limit liability company (LLC). The exciting new direction would be starting your new business in manufacturing. When we have the intention, it is always a complete process from thought to action to completion. All intention (processes) starts with a thought. Before you act, you should express excitement. The excitement moves you into action. Because this is an exciting activity, it will be easy to complete the task at hand.

    d) My affirmations

    Write down a few affirmations that will generate excitement when you say them.

Affirmations are tricky because there has to be coordination between the thought of saying the affirmation, believing what the conscious mind says, and the action that will be taken. A person can claim the affirmation, "I am a multi-millionaire"; however, if being a millionaire is not in the person's belief system, it will never work. The ego mind will be quick to point out, "No, you're not!"

In the beginning, find affirmations that will lead you toward where you want to go without the ego mind questioning their validity. The affirmations must a have good energy feel when you say them. Good examples are, "I am going to be wealthy" and "I am a talented photographer." Be sure to associate genius emotions with the affirmations. I like to work with affirmations in meditation because that is when I'm more in the alpha (relaxed) state of mind. I have easier access to higher mind and the imagination to be included in the process.

e) Value system(s) that supports this activity

Write down the supporting value systems for this activity. The supporting value system should reflect your top three value systems from your exciting value systems list. If you establish exciting new directions with value systems in the lower-tier group of your exciting value systems list, chances are that you won't accomplish your goals and your new direction. Any value systems that are in the lower half of your list will not get as much attention as those in the upper list. One of the reasons that goals do not work is that the goals do not match what is valued most in one's life.

f) What are the first few steps to take?

To begin the process of breaking old energy patterns and unwanted activities, as a first step, spend time understanding your value systems. We are bombarded with thousands of behaviors, belief systems, and true/false programming. You will find that there are many unwanted behaviors, beliefs that we didn't choose or handed down from parents, and past generations of family members. These unwanted beliefs and behaviors are in all of the value systems. We are that complex. However, there's simplicity about us. Simplicities have its advantages.

Make a list of a few simple steps that could change the course to a new and exciting life.

Understanding how you spend your time on Earth is a big deal!

—Keith Thompson

LIST YOUR VALUE SYSTEMS ACCORDING TO THE IMPORTANCE

Health, Career and Personal Development, Wealth and Financial, Family, Social, Spiritual, Emotional and Mental, and Physical

1.	
2.	
3.	
4.	
5.	
6.	
7.	
8.	

Date: _____

WEEKDAY AND WEEKEND ACTIVITIES I DO

Value systems: Career and Personal Development, Emotional and Mental, Family, Financial and Wealth, Health, Physical, Social, Spiritual

e) Check	b) Weekday Activities	b) Hours	c) Value System	d) Connected Value System

Weekend activities I do

Value systems: Career and Personal Development, Emotional and Mental, Family, Financial and Wealth, Health, Physical, Social, Spiritual

Check	Saturday Activities	Hours	Value System	Connected Value System

WEEKEND ACTIVITIES I DO Date:

Check	Sunday Activities	Hours	Value System	Connected Value System

TOTAL UP THE HOURS

➤ Health -   One week

Weekday hours		Weekday hours x 5	
		Weekend hours	
Total weekend and weekday health hours			

➤ Career and Personal Development

Weekday hours		Weekday hours x 5	
		Weekend hours	
Total weekend and weekday Career and Personal Development hours			

➤ Financial and Wealth

Weekday hours		Weekday hours x 5	
		Weekend hours	
Total weekend and weekday Financial and Wealth hours			

➤ Family

Weekday hours		Weekday hours x 5	
		Weekend hours	
Total weekend and weekday Family hours			

➤ Social

Weekday hours		Weekday hours x 5	
		Weekend hours	
Total weekend and weekday Social hours			

➤ Spiritual

Weekday hours		Weekday hours x 5	
		Weekend hours	
Total weekend and weekday Spiritual hours			

➤ Emotional and Mental

Weekday hours		Weekday hours x 5	
		Weekend hours	
Total weekend and weekday Emotional and Mental hours			

➤ Physical

Weekday hours		Weekday hours x 5	
		Weekend hours	
Total weekend and weekday Physical hours			

DAILY VALUE SYSTEMS COMPARISON

Value System from Exercise #1	Daily Activity Value Systems
1.	
2.	
3.	
4.	
5.	
6.	
7.	
8.	

Note: How did you do? Does the current order of your value systems match up with your daily value systems? In many cases, the most important values in peoples' lives do not match up with their daily activities. It is important to realize how we spend our value of time! The goal is to find out how to live your life according to your genius values instead of living life according to someone else's values.

MY EXCITING WEEKDAY ACTIVITIES—THINGS I WOULD LOVE TO DO

Weekly Activities	Hours	Value System	Connecting Value System

My exciting Saturday activities: things I would love to do

Saturday Activities	Hours	Value System	Connecting Value System

My exciting Sunday activities: things I would love to do

Sunday Activities	Hours	Value System	Connecting Value System

ORDER OF MY EXCITING VALUE SYSTEM

1.	
2.	
3.	
4.	
5.	
6.	
7.	
8.	

Date:_____

MY EXCITING DIRECTION EXAMPLE

My Exciting Direction
a)   **Exciting activity:** To see all the wonders of the world.
b)   **Vision(s): In this activity write down what you see in your imagination.** I see myself traveling to New York and visiting Niagara Falls, studying about the Druids and visiting Stonehenge, and studying about Machu Pichu and making plans to travel there.
c)   Intention(s): **Intention begins with thought, continues with action, and ends with the completion of the task! I will start my research the next time I'm on the internet and will set potential dates to travel to my favorite locations.**
d)   **Affirmation(s): An affirmation is a positive assertion. Use "I am" or "I have"!** I am a world traveler.
e)   **Value system that supports the activity:** Spiritual

f) **What are the first few steps to take?**

1. I will pick seven places to travel to.

    _____

2. I will do research on all seven places. _____

3. I will set potential dates for travel to all locations. _____

My Exciting Direction

a) **Exciting Activity:**

b) Vision(s): In this activity, write down what you see in your imagination.

c) **Intention(s): Intention begins with thought, continues with action, and ends with the completion of the task!**

d) **Affirmation(s): An affirmation is a positive assertion. Use "I am" or "I have"!**

e) **Value system that supports the activity:**

f) **What are the first few steps to take?**

1. _____

2. _____

3. _____

My Exciting Direction

a) **Exciting activity:**

b) **Vision(s): In this activity, write down what you see in your imagination.**

c) **Intention(s): Intention begins with thought, continues with action, and ends with the completion of the task!**

d) **Affirmation(s): An affirmation is a positive assertion. Use "I am" or "I have"!**

e) **Value system that supports the activity:**

f) **What are the first few steps to take?**

1. _____

2. _____

3. _____

My Exciting Direction
a) **Exciting activity:**
b) **Vision(s): In this activity, write down what you see in your imagination.**
c) **Intention(s): Intention begins with thought, continues with action, and ends with the completion of the task!**
d) **Affirmation(s): An affirmation is a positive assertion. Use "I am" or "I have"!**
e) **Value system that supports the activity:**
f) **What are the first few steps to take?**

1. _____

2. _____

3. _____

Sign and Date: _____

CHAPTER 6

THE TRANSITION

The Transition is a guide consisting of three major exercises to assist you in moving out of negative conditions in your value systems and into positive conditions. Whether the energy we experience is positive or negative, it comes from only one source. Free will makes it possible to experience both positive and negative energies. You can be a product of the genius mind or the ego mind.

Let's use water as an analogy. Imagine running water in a sink. Only the cold water is on. The cold is at one end of the spectrum of water. Let's call the cold water negative energy. Now let's introduce hot water. Hot water is the positive side of the spectrum. As we introduce more hot water into the cold water, the energy changes and the water become warmer. Let's say the warmth of the water is 98.6. We can say this is the temperature of balanced water when hot- and cold-water energies are equal.

When we are balanced, we can be the observer. We can feel both positive (hot) and negative (cold) energies. One energy doesn't dominate over the other energy. When we look at this from an emotional perspective, the emotional filters are gone because there's no domination. It has been my observation that, when I see both sides of the spectrum, I see more opportunities and I can make clearer choices that lead to genius emotions.

As the positive energy continues to heat up, the water gets hot, turns into steam, and begins to disperse into the air. The water has transformed and changed its reality with positive energy. The dispersed energy in the air now becomes new choices.

On the other hand, if the negative energy increases, the water continues to slow down as it gets colder. The water begins to transform and turns into ice. The water has solidified and is now stagnant. The negative energy is now a negative emotion.

The dispersed transformed positive energy can be used to establish new emotions that support genius lifestyle. The solidified negative energy operates at a low frequency, and the negative emotions are stuck in place with little or no movement.

When our emotions are cold and stagnant, we are in a stuck state. This is the inability to change unwanted conditions. The goals of the transition exercises are to transform negative energy into positive energy, to know your elements that include your eight value systems, to establish a body/mind/genius connection, and to set genius desires in all your value systems.

EIGHT IMPORTANT ELEMENTS

The eight elements combine to form the driving engine that brings awareness and discovery to your value system journey and your genius code. The purpose of this information is to help you realize when you are in your different elements. It's of great value to know when you're in a specific value system or any of the other elements. When you know you're in the ego mind, you can quickly make the change back to the genius element. When you realize you are more than a physical body, the genius mind will be more present. The conscious mind will begin to make more genius decisions. With genius decisions, the other elements are alive because of the element of excitement.

- **Value systems:** There will be times when a certain value system will demand your attention. For example, your goals and desires are in Career and Personal Development, and you are engaged and working to your desires. Suddenly, a family matter arises. Follow the value system that requires the most attention. The value systems rotate often; that is why it's a good idea to have goals and desires in all the value systems.

- **The genius mind:** Follow the genius emotions you defined in the chapter Emotions of the Genius Mind and the Ego Mind. Look for situations in your life where joy and happiness are and build on those conditions. The genius mind represents all the good about who we are. The genius mind can connect to the higher mind and bring in the necessary tools and information for manifestation. The genius mind can use tools like universal laws. The genius mind represents the best of us in each of the value systems. The genius mind can heal anything that is out of balance with each value systems. Mental and physical work is required. For mental work, the genius mind will be in charge of making decisions. For physical work, create an alignment with the mental work to promote healing the physical body and bring in light.

- **The ego mind:** The ego mind is in complete opposition to the genius mind and always seeks to do us harm. If you are ill, you owe it to yourself to look for ego emotions. The ego mind may be responsible for both mental and physical illnesses we experience and any disharmony within each value system. The higher mind doesn't recognize the ego mind because it doesn't operate in its low frequency. Make it a choice to seek higher awareness. When we use the ego mind, we are in a state of illusion because of the low vibration. False emotion/evidence appearing real (FEAR) is the ego mind. Being hard on yourself is the ego mind.

- **The thinker:** The thinker has the power to choose. We always can choose to use the genius mind or the ego mind. We can choose which emotions to use such as love, joy, and happiness. The thinker also can expand upon what it sees in the imagination by making the connection to the higher mind.

- **The feeler:** The feeler, under the control of the thinker, has the power to move in and out of all value system and the subconscious mind by creating and removing associations with the emotions. The feeler is the energy connector from thoughts to emotions. The feeler can create and remove addictions and can create a life full of passion and joy in the creative process. The emotions from memories lock our behaviors in place to repeat life conditions over and over again. The way we react to the events in our physical world plays a big role in how we feel.

  Ask yourself the question, "How do I feel?" This question can expose a host of emotions that are currently being played out. Removing negative emotions is the key to living life with our highest excitements. The feeler is energy. The thinker and the feeler can turn energy into emotions by thinking of past events. The emotions of past events are one of the reasons we can't move forward to the present moment. When we encounter a family member or someone who has harmed us, we revert to that past event with the emotions intact. What are the emotions that keep me in a stagnate state? Questions like this are a good ones to ask. When an unwanted emotion pops up, command yourself to "Stop. Change. New direction." Stop sending negative feelings to that past event. Use the emotional balancing system to incorporate genius thinking and feelings to the situation.

A great way to be in the present moment is to be the observer, be engaged with what you're doing in each moment, and be in excitement. The present moment is a great place to recognize your great spirit and all the wonderful things you're doing.

The way we project to the future with our feelings becomes important. We want to be sure to project good emotions into the future. The feeler starts to get feedback from what we are creating. No longer use the feeler to project negative emotions. Projecting fear of the future is the ego mind, and it creates illusions.

It has been my experience the feeler connects to everything.

- **The observer:** Being the observer is a powerful tool used by the thinker and the conscious mind to observe the subconscious mind's emotions, past events, and current events. During an event, the observer can objectively witness all the nuances and action taking place at a higher level because the observer has removed all the emotions (filters). You can use the observer in your current situations to view emotions and thoughts being played out in your mind. Using the observer is a great way to change or adjust belief systems. Using the observer is also a great way to neutralize unwanted emotions. When the observer and the feeler are used together, you can spot an ego emotion faster. You can use the observer to spot any unwanted emotions, like fears and doubt of self. The process of neutralizing an ego emotion begins with the command "Stop. Change. New direction."

- **The believer:** The believer is the crown of the physical world. The thinker, the feeler, and emotions feed fuel to the believer. The believer plays a role in every value system and every belief within each value. For beginners, some belief systems are controlled by the ego mind. As I mentioned before, under the Ego Mind, there will be fears and self-doubts. I won't mention any self-doubts or fears because recognizing them is part of self-discovery. But know this—if you're not living your desires in all of your value systems, chances are fear (false evidence appearing real) is operating.

Because the genius mind operates at a higher vibration, when the genius mind uses the believer, it has access to higher levels of mind like higher mind, spirit, universal laws, the soul, and beyond. Of course, this all depends on what your beliefs are.

- What am I thinking?
- How am I feeling?
- What are my emotions?
- What do I believe, and why do I believe this?

These are the questions to ask in each value system when a belief is under observation. You create new belief systems by diving deeper into your mission statements in each of your genius value systems.

- **Living by your highest excitement:** Excitements are the emotions that bring joy, peace, happiness, and all the genius emotions you've identified. Living life by your highest excitement can be as simple as reading a book or going for a walk. It can also be living life beyond your highest expectations or doing the things you always dreamed of doing. Living life from a genius perspective, with excitement, intent, and purpose is a worthy goal to obtain. To start, pick out an exciting event every day.

CONNECTING TO THE EIGHT ELEMENTS

Knowing if a value system is drawing in genius energy or ego energy is an important step in healing and accelerating your genius changes in beliefs. Learning to become the believer gives power to the genius mind. If there's a value system that needs to change, work on that value system exclusively. Use the Define Genius Value Systems and all the exercises in this section to assist you. Allow the feeler to move through each of the elements within that value system. Be the observer often within the value systems and discover where the excitements and holdbacks are. Let your genius mind alert you when it's time to move on to the next value system.

The following questions will assist you in your journey and begin the process of connecting the elements in your life.

1. **Is my _____ value mostly controlled by the genius mind or the ego mind?**

   Rate where you think, feel, and believe your value systems are currently. Be the observer and see how the genius mind and ego mind are involved in your values. Use both sides of the scale to represent the genius mind and the ego mind. Make sure the two lines equal to ten on the scale. To increase the genius mind, begin the process of removing elements of the ego mind.

1. **Is my *health* value mostly controlled by the genius mind or the ego mind?**

   Genius mind_____

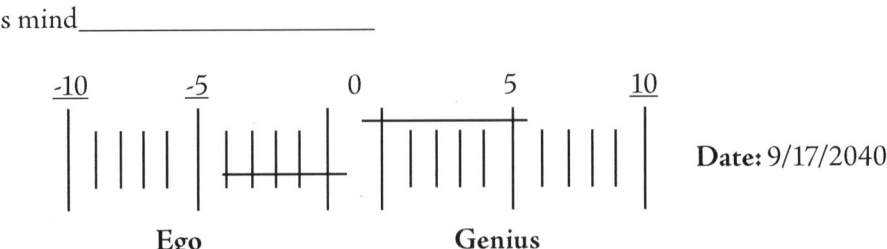

   Date: 9/17/2040

2. **What are my genius thoughts about my _____ value?**

This exercise discovers where genius thoughts are. Use the following steps to discover genius thoughts. The steps will guide you further along in the processes. The steps do not fall in a particular order.

- Once you find a genius thought, look for the associated emotions. They should be in some form of excitement.
- When you experience excitement, you can create new belief systems around the excitement.
- Create your genius plan. Celebrate your new plan. You can place your new genius plan in the Things I Desire section.

The key elements to use in all of the "what are my genius _____ about my _____ value, exercises": the thinker, the genius, the feeler, the observer, the believer, living life by your highest excitement

2a. **What are my ego thoughts about my _____ value?**

This exercise helps you discover where those ego thoughts are coming from, discover the associated emotions, and discover the associated belief systems. An ego thought example: "you make me sick."

- Once you discover an ego thought, follow it to the ego's feelings.
- When you discover an ego emotion, follow it to the belief.
- When you discover an ego belief system, be sure to celebrate the findings.
- Make new choices and decisions using the genius mind. You can use this newfound energy in the Things I Desire section under Undesirable.

The key elements to use in all of the "what are my ego _____ about my _____ value, exercises": the thinker, the genius mind, the ego mind, the feeler, the observer, the believer

3. **What are my values that make up my _____ (value)?**

Multiple values make up our specific value system. In this exercise, identify your values within each value system. For example, your value is that you will work every day to support your family. This example touches on three value systems: Family, Career, and Financial. If you have value systems like this, the goal is to make sure each of the value systems is in alignment with the others so you can work in the genius realm. If you are in a career you do not like, that could disrupt the other two value systems and cause the ego mind emotions to play out through all three systems.

Part of the discovery is to realize that the genius mind and the ego mind have been used by the thinker to establish values, emotions, and belief systems. You may find most value systems and belief systems were handed down by your parents. If the thinker has used the genius and the ego, confusion will set in the subconscious mind and affect that value system. Because the genius and the ego use different emotions and thought processes, there will always be conflict. Some people have value systems mostly controlled by their ego minds. The ego mind is always in a confused state of being and has no way of finding a solution. If you ask, the subconscious mind will find any problems in your values with the help of genius thinking and intervention.

Use all the elements to explore this one.

4. **What am I observing most about my _____ value?**

Do a life review of each of your value systems. Go back to the earliest time in your life you can refer to that value. Look for key players who influenced you in your value system. Bringing in awareness about your value system is the objective of this exercise.

My example falls under Career and Personal Development, Social, Family, and Financial and Wealth. I used personal development as my primary focus. I was about twelve at the time. My next-door neighbor's dad worked at a bowling alley in the early mornings on the weekends. They would invite me to go along and help with vacuuming the carpets, sweeping, and mopping the floors. We would arrive at the bowling alley at 3:00 in the morning. I don't remember getting paid money for it. But it was a lot of fun! We would work for about three hours and finish at about six in the morning. The bowling alley didn't open until nine. The restaurant served buffets in the evenings, and there were always plenty of leftovers. The first thing we would do was enjoy our feast. There were all the meats we could ask for along with all kinds of veggies, cakes, pastries, and ice cream. After the feast, we would head over to pool tables and shoot about four games of eight ball. Our next stop would be the bowling lanes! Bowling first thing in morning seemed so cool to me back then. My father used to be a good bowler.

The key elements to use in the observer exercise: the feeler, the observer, and the believer

5. **What are my genius feelings about my _____ value?**

All genius feelings come from a higher connection. From the "journey" perspective, it is genius to be aware of all your values and realize those values come from a higher place. When you realize that you are greater than you think, you bring in humbleness and open up room for greater growth.

5a. **What are my ego feelings about my _____ value?**

Identifying ego feelings is equally as important as finding genius feelings. When you discover an ego feeling, decide at that moment to continue forward by sending energy with your thoughts to those feelings. If you don't, stop entertaining the feelings immediately.

6.   **What are my genius beliefs about my _____ value?**

The best place to start is to form the belief system that everyone is a genius and all things are possible. Keep building on your beliefs. A genius belief system can be made of many facets. For health values, you can incorporate beliefs about drinking lots of water, keeping your body alkaline, spending one hour every day in meditation, going for three-mile walks three times a week, and eating plenty of fruits and vegetables. All of these items can make up a genius health value system.

6a. **What are my ego beliefs about my _____ value?**

Your physical reality will change when you identify ego belief and change it into genius belief. Removing FEAR (false evidence appearing real) out of every value system is the path to living life by your highest excitements.

7.   **Living life by my highest excitement _____**

Make a list of your highest excitements in each of your value systems. What do you see yourself doing and experiencing? The highest excitement can range from going for a walk or reading a good book to seeing all the wonders of the world. Think of ten different exciting things to experience in each value systems.

HEALTH VALUES—CONNECTING TO THE EIGHT ELEMENTS

1. **Is my health mostly controlled by the genius mind or the ego mind?**

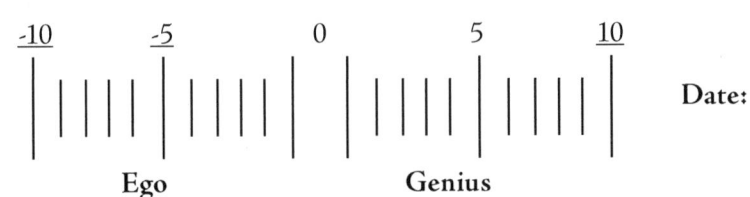

Date:

Ego   Genius

2. **What are my genius thoughts about my Health values?**

+ _____

_____

+ _____

_____

+ _____

_____

2a. What are my ego thoughts about my Health values?

+ _____

_____

+ _____

_____

+ _____

_____

3. **What are the values that make up my Health values?**

+ _____

_____

+ _____

_____

+ _____

_____

4. **What am I observing most about my Health values?**

+ _____

_____

+ _____

_____

+ _____

_____

5. **What are my genius feelings about my Health values?**

+ _____

_____

+ _____

_____

+ _____

_____

5a. **What are my ego feelings about my Health values?**

+ _____

_____

+ _____

_____

◆ _____

_____

6. **What are my genius beliefs about my Health values?**

◆ _____

_____

◆ _____

_____

◆ _____

_____

6a. **What are my ego beliefs about my Health values?**

◆ _____

_____

◆ _____

_____

◆ _____

_____

Act:

7. **I am living life by my highest excitement with regard to health.**

◆ _____

_____

◆ _____

_____

◆ _____

◆ _____

◆ _____

◆ _____

◆ _____

◆ _____

◆ _____

◆ _____

CAREER AND PERSONAL DEVELOPMENT VALUES—CONNECTING TO THE EIGHT ELEMENTS

1. Are my career values mostly controlled by the genius mind or the ego mind?

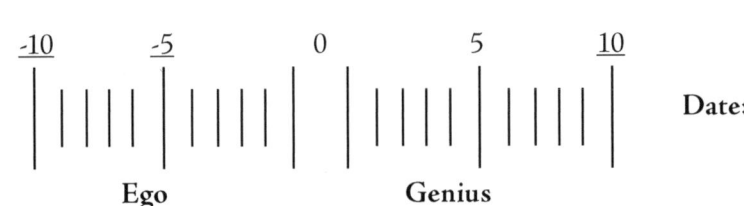

Date:

Ego   Genius

2. What are my genius thoughts about my Career and Personal Development?

• _____

_____

• _____

_____

• _____

_____

2a. What are my ego thoughts about my Career and Personal Development?

• _____

_____

• _____

_____

• _____

_____

3. **What are my values about my career? Am I doing what I love to do?**

    Yes _____ No _____

    - _____

    _____

    - _____

    _____

    - _____

    _____

4. **What am I observing about my Career and Personal Development?**

    - _____

    _____

    - _____

    _____

    - _____

    _____

5. **What are my genius feelings about my Career and Personal Development?**

    - _____

    _____

    - _____

    _____

    - _____

    _____

5a. What are my ego feelings about my Career and Personal Development?

+ _____
  _____

+ _____
  _____

+ _____
  _____

6. **What are my genius beliefs about my Career and Personal Development?**

+ _____
  _____

+ _____
  _____

+ _____
  _____

6a. What are my ego beliefs about my Career and Personal Development?

+ _____
  _____

+ _____
  _____

Act:

7. **What are the exciting things I am seeing about my Career and Personal Development?**

- _____

  _____

- _____

  _____

- _____

  _____

- _____

  _____

- _____

  _____

- _____

  _____

- _____

  _____

- _____

  _____

- _____

  _____

Emotional and Mental Values—Connecting to the Eight Elements

1. Are my emotions mostly controlled by the genius mind or the ego mind?

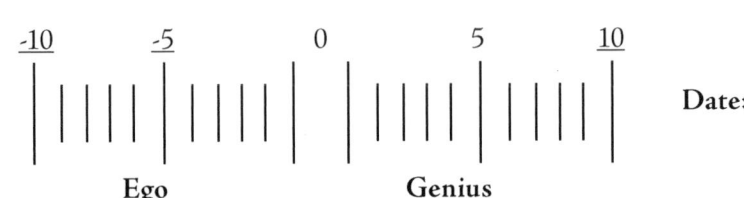

2. What are my genius thoughts about my Emotional and Mental values?

    • _____

       _____

    • _____

       _____

    • _____

       _____

2a. What are my ego thoughts about my Emotional and Mental values?

    • _____

       _____

    • _____

       _____

+ _____

_____

_____

3. **What are my values about my emotions?**

   + Do I love the person I am? Yes _____ No _____

   + _____

   _____

   _____

   + _____

   _____

   _____

   + _____

   _____

   _____

4. **What am I observing about my emotions?**

   + _____

   _____

   _____

   + _____

   _____

   _____

   + _____

   _____

   _____

5.   What are my genius feelings about my Emotional and Mental values?

    ◆ _____

       _____

       _____

    ◆ _____

       _____

       _____

    ◆ _____

       _____

       _____

5a. What are my ego feelings about my Emotional and Mental values?

    ◆ _____

       _____

       _____

    ◆ _____

       _____

       _____

    ◆ _____

       _____

6.   What are my genius beliefs about my Emotional and Mental values?

    ◆ _____

       _____

＊ _____

_____

_____

_____

＊ _____

_____

_____

6a. What are my ego beliefs about my Emotional and Mental_values?

＊ _____

_____

_____

＊ _____

_____

_____

＊ _____

_____

_____

Act:

7. **What are the exciting things I am doing with my Emotional and Mental values?**

+ _____

_____

_____

+ _____

_____

_____

+ _____

_____

_____

_____

+ _____

_____

_____

+ _____

_____

_____

+ _____

_____

_____

+ _____

_____

_____

+ _____

_____

_____

+ _____

_____

_____

+ _____

_____

_____

FAMILY VALUES—CONNECTING TO THE EIGHT ELEMENTS

1. **Are my family values mostly controlled by the genius mind or the ego mind?**

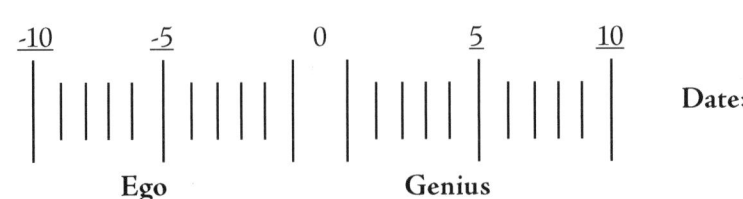

Date:

Ego Genius

2. **What are my genius thoughts about my Family values?**

  * _____

    _____

    _____

    _____

  * _____

    _____

    _____

    _____

  * _____

    _____

    _____

    _____

2a. What are my ego thoughts about my Family values?

  * _____

    _____

    _____

    _____

  * _____

    _____

    _____

+ _____

_____

_____

3. **What are my values for my family?**

   + Do I love all members of my family?

   Yes _____ No _____

   + _____

   _____

   _____

   + _____

   _____

   _____

   + _____

   _____

   _____

4. **What am I observing about my Family values?**

   + _____

   _____

   _____

   + _____

   _____

   _____

   + _____

_____

_____

5.   **What are my genius feelings about my Family values?**

   ♦   _____

   _____

   _____

   ♦   _____

   _____

   _____

   ♦   _____

   _____

   _____

5a. What are my ego feelings about my Family values?

   ♦   _____

   _____

   _____

   ♦   _____

   _____

   ♦   _____

   _____

   _____

6. **What are my genius beliefs about my Family values?**

- ◆ _____

  _____

  _____

- ◆ _____

  _____

  _____

- ◆ _____

  _____

  _____

6a. **What are my ego beliefs about my Family values?**

- ◆ _____

  _____

  _____

- ◆ _____

  _____

  _____

- ◆ _____

  _____

  _____

Act:

7. **What are the exciting things I am doing with my family?**

+ _____

_____

_____

+ _____

_____

_____

+ _____

_____

_____

+ _____

_____

_____

+ _____

_____

_____

+ _____

_____

_____

+ _____

_____

_____

+ _____

_____

_____

+ _____

_____

_____

+ _____

_____

_____

Financial and Wealth—Connecting to the Eight Elements

1.   **Are my finances mostly controlled by the genius mind or the ego mind?**

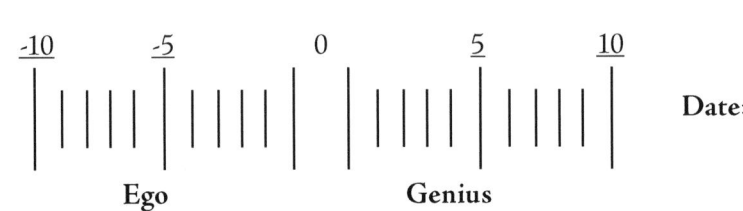

Date:

2.   **What are my genius thoughts about my Financial and Wealth values?**

+   _____

    _____

    _____

    _____

+   _____

    _____

    _____

    _____

+   _____

    _____

    _____

    _____

2a. What are my ego thoughts about my Financial and Wealth values?

+   _____

    _____

    _____

    _____

+   _____

    _____

    _____

+ _____

_____

_____

_____

3. **What are my values about my Financial and Wealth values?**

+ _____

_____

_____

+ _____

_____

_____

_____

+ _____

_____

_____

_____

4. **What am I observing about my Financial and Wealth values?**

+ _____

_____

_____

+ _____

_____

_____

+ _____

_____

_____

5. **What are my genius feelings about my Financial and Wealth values?**

 + _____
   _____
   _____

 + _____
   _____
   _____

 + _____
   _____
   _____

5a. **What are my ego feelings about my Financial and Wealth values?**

 + _____
   _____
   _____

 + _____
   _____
   _____

 + _____
   _____
   _____

6. **What are my genius beliefs about my Financial and Wealth values?**

 + _____
   _____

_____

+   _____

_____

_____

_____

+   _____

_____

_____

6a. What are my ego beliefs about my Financial and Wealth values?

+   _____

_____

_____

+   _____

_____

_____

+   _____

_____

_____

Act:

7. **What are the exciting things I am doing about my financial values?**

+   _____

_____

_____

- _____
  _____
  _____

- _____
  _____
  _____

- _____
  _____
  _____

- _____
  _____
  _____

- _____
  _____
  _____

- _____
  _____
  _____

- _____
  _____
  _____

♦ _____

_____

_____

♦ _____

_____

_____

Physical Values—Connecting to the Eight Elements

1. Are my physical values and environment mostly controlled by the genius mind or the ego mind?

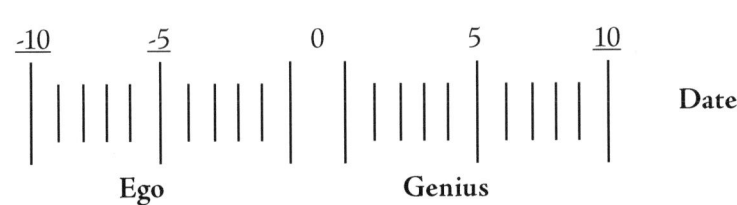

Ego   Genius

Date:

2. What are my genius thoughts about my Physical values?

    ◆ _____

_____

_____

    ◆ _____

_____

_____

    ◆ _____

_____

_____

2a. What are my ego thoughts about my Physical values?

    ◆ _____

_____

_____

    ◆ _____

_____

_____

> ◆ _____
>
> _____
>
> _____

3. **What are my values about my physical world?**

> ◆ _____
>
> _____
>
> _____
>
> ◆ _____
>
> _____
>
> _____
>
> ◆ _____
>
> _____
>
> _____

Do I love my body? Yes _____ No _____

Do I love my environment? Yes _____ No _____

4. **What am I observing about my Physical values?**

> ◆ _____
>
> _____
>
> _____
>
> ◆ _____
>
> _____
>
> _____
>
> ◆ _____

_____

_____

5.   **What are my genius feelings about my Physical values?**

   •   _____

       _____

       _____

   •   _____

       _____

       _____

   •   _____

       _____

       _____

5a. What are my ego feelings about my Physical values?

   •   _____

       _____

       _____

   •   _____

       _____

       _____

   •   _____

       _____

       _____

6. **What are my genius beliefs about my Physical values?**

    + _____

       _____

       _____

    + _____

       _____

       _____

    + _____

       _____

       _____

6a. **What are my ego beliefs about my Physical values?**

    + _____

       _____

       _____

    + _____

       _____

       _____

    + _____

       _____

       _____

Act:

7. **What are the exciting things I am doing with my Physical values and environment?**

+ _____

_____

_____

+ _____

_____

_____

+ _____

_____

_____

+ _____

_____

_____

+ _____

_____

_____

+ _____

_____

_____

+ _____

_____

_____

+ _____

_____

_____

+ _____

_____

_____

+ _____

_____

_____

SOCIAL CALUES—CONNECTING TO THE EIGHT ELEMENTS

1. Are my social values and environment mostly controlled by the genius mind or the ego mind? _____

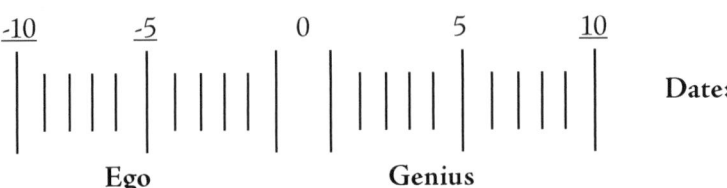

Ego   Genius   Date:

2. What are my genius thoughts about my Social values?

* _____

_____

_____

* _____

_____

_____

* _____

_____

_____

2a. What are my ego thoughts about my Social values?

* _____

_____

_____

* _____

_____

_____

* _____

_____

_____

3. **What are my values in my social world?**

    ♦   _____

        _____

        _____

    ♦   _____

        _____

        _____

    ♦   _____

        _____

        _____

4. **What am I observing about my Social values?**

    ♦   _____

        _____

        _____

    ♦   _____

        _____

        _____

    ♦   _____

        _____

        _____

5. What are my genius feelings about my Social values?

    • _____

       _____

       _____

    • _____

       _____

       _____

    • _____

       _____

       _____

5a. What are my ego feelings about my Social values?

    • _____

       _____

       _____

    • _____

       _____

       _____

    • _____

       _____

       _____

6. What are my genius beliefs about my Social values?

    • _____

       _____

_____

+ _____

_____

_____

_____

+ _____

_____

_____

6a. What are my ego beliefs about my Social values?

+ _____

_____

_____

_____

+ _____

_____

_____

_____

+ _____

_____

_____

Act:

7. **What are the exciting things I am doing socially?**

+ _____

_____

_____

+ _____

- _____

- _____

- _____

- _____

- _____

- _____

Spiritual Values—Connecting to the Eight Elements

1. Are my spiritual values mostly controlled by the genius mind or the ego mind?

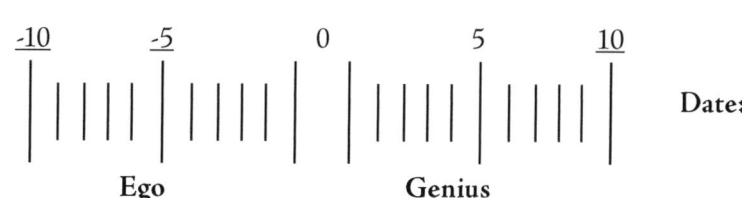

Date:

Ego   Genius

2. What are my genius thoughts about my Spiritual values?

*   _____

    _____

    _____

*   _____

    _____

    _____

*   _____

    _____

    _____

2a. What are my ego thoughts about my Spiritual values?

*   _____

    _____

    _____

*   _____

    _____

    _____

+ _____
  _____
  _____

3. **What are my values in my spiritual world?**

+ _____
  _____
  _____

+ _____
  _____
  _____

+ _____
  _____
  _____

4. **What am I observing about my Spiritual values?**

+ _____
  _____
  _____

+ _____
  _____
  _____

+ _____
  _____
  _____

5.   What are my genius feelings about my Spiritual values?

 •   _____

     _____

     _____

 •   _____

     _____

     _____

 •   _____

     _____

     _____

5a. What are my ego feelings about my Spiritual values?

 •   _____

     _____

     _____

 •   _____

     _____

     _____

 •   _____

     _____

     _____

6.   What are my genius beliefs about my Spiritual values?

 •   _____

     _____

◆ _____

_____

_____

_____

◆ _____

_____

_____

6a. What are my ego beliefs about my Spiritual values?

◆ _____

_____

_____

_____

◆ _____

_____

_____

_____

◆ _____

_____

_____

_____

_____

_____

Act:

What are the exciting things I am doing with my Spiritual values?

- _____

  _____

  _____

- _____

  _____

  _____

- _____

  _____

  _____

- _____

  _____

  _____

- _____

  _____

  _____

- _____

  _____

  _____

- _____

◆ _____

_____

_____

Sign and Date:_____

CHAPTER 7

THE EMOTIONAL BALANCING SYSTEM

The emotional balancing system is an effective tool for transforming negative emotions into positive emotions. By transforming your emotions, you'll transform all your outcomes. The emotional balancing system is a great tool to use for any emotional challenges within the value systems. Anyone suffering from any illness or family dysfunction should use this tool.

In this exercise, any illness listed falls under the Mind category because the illness is part of a creative process. The emotions are part of the Mind category process as well.

Under the category of Body, list only the things you put into your body. In this exercise, we are addressing what is coming from the mind and what we are physically putting into the body.

List one condition per exercise and list up to four negative emotions tied to the condition or what you are currently experiencing. For example, you got dumped from a long-term relationship. The second example is, you're faced with a serious illness, and you're overwhelmed by the news. For both the exercises, list the ego emotions you were experiencing then and are experiencing now.

The scale is your emotional grid. List the type of emotions you are experiencing. Draw a line up to the number that represents where you are emotionally.

On the right-hand side of the paper list the positive side of the emotion, an opposite equivalent of the negative emotion. The objective is to have the gridline go in a positive direction. For example, a negative emotion would be frustration, and it's at 8.5 in a negative direction. Create an emotion to move the line in a positive direction; an example is the emotion of peace.

If a person, place, or situation is tied to an emotion, write it in the space provided. The goal and the objective is to make peace with the situation and condition.

USING THE EMOTIONAL BALANCING SYSTEM

Examples

Mind: Use this space if there's an illness: Write down the name of the illness. Do not use "I have" here! Remember, when we use the word *I*, we are announcing the spirit and turning on the subconscious mind recorder and activating our belief systems. If you about to write "I have _____ (illness)" stop it immediately!

Ischemic heart disease _____

List the ego emotions you're experiencing. *Anger, frustration, dislike, and resentment*

_____

What are you putting into your body? List suspected things you are putting in your body to assist in the emotions and illnesses. For example: Cigarettes, recreational and pharmaceutical drugs, alcohol, caffeine, toxic foods (junk foods), too much food of any kind. Do not use the word *I* here either!

Smoking cigarettes, eating fried and fatty foods, using opioids, and drinking lots of coffee.

Value System(s): List the value systems most affected by the conditions.

Health, emotional, financial, spiritual.

Type of negative emotion Transform into a positive emotion

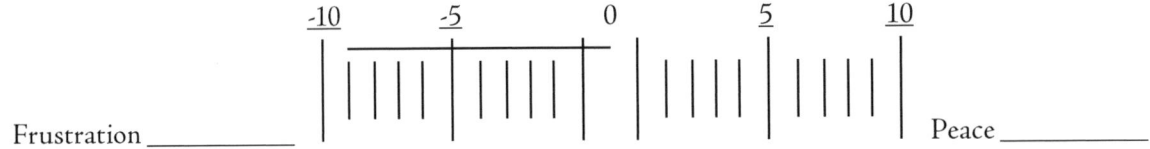

Frustration _____   Peace _____

Name a person, place, or thing associated with this emotion.

Father _____

Situation: *He said, I wasn't worth a hill of dried up beans.*

_____

Type of negative emotion Transform into a positive emotion

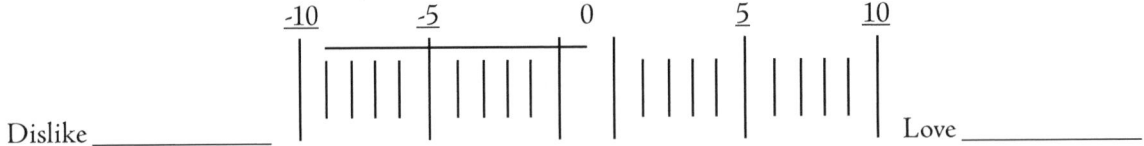

Dislike _____   Love _____

Name a person, place or thing associated with this emotion. *Going to work* _____

Situation: *I dislike what I'm doing on my job.* _____

What foods and drugs are you are putting into your body associated with the ego's emotions and conditions?

Foods and drugs	Ego's emotions or conditions
Cigarettes	Frustration, anxiety, stress
Doritos	Anger
Cookies	Sugar high
Hamburgers, french fries, milkshakes	Make me feel better
Opioids	Pain in my life
Pizza	Comfort

A Transition Idea with Foods

When it comes to dealing with foods and drugs, I recommend doing your research. Hire a nutritionist or a health coach and talk to a doctor you trust if you need someone to help you remove drugs from your system.

Work on transforming your ego emotions into genius emotions in relationship to eating food. Finding the ego emotions will take awareness on your part. If you know that the foods you're eating are junk, immediately check your emotions to see what's playing out in your mind that drew you to those foods.

Food is energy that turns into fuel for the body. When looking at food from an energetic point of view, you can see that packaged foods contain little life while freshly picked foods from a vine or a tree are full of life. Our bodies tell us if the food it just received creates a high or low vibration. The feeler will let us know immediately. And we can tell if we are eating the right foods by simply looking in the mirror. This isn't a mystery. We all eat food every day.

Consider this: if you're sitting down to eat and watching the evening or local news on tell-a-vision, you are watching and listening to a vibration that may lower your frequencies through negative emotions, such as killings and violent actions. Pay attention to this behavior because, unknowingly, it may put you in a negative mood during your meal.

Pay attention to what you're putting into your mind and what you think about when you eat. If you are having a conversation at the dinner table that involves negative comments about someone or other negative subjects, stop it instantaneously. The same goes with entertaining negative thoughts while eating. Having negative thoughts while you eat is a double whammy that involves the activity in both your mind and body.

Remember, foods and thoughts are energy! I believe there's a correlation between the two, the combination results in rapid manifestation of our thoughts in our world. This correlation works in the genius realm as well as the ego realm.

Just imagine what genius emotions and healthy foods can do for our bodies. Remember, emotions produce chemicals in the body called neuropeptides. Positive emotions and healthy foods are a winning combination for health. I make it a practice when eating alone to play high vibrating music like wealth and abundance music, meditative music. Sometimes I maintain silence in the house so I can think about positive things. Sometimes I must work at it.

"As we embrace the emotion ahead of the environment, we are signaling the gene ahead of the environment." (D. J. Dispenza 2019). Eating food is a present-moment event. Use your genius thoughts and emotions to visualize a current event or create a future event while eating. If you choose to visualize the future while eating, project beautiful and wonderful things for yourself.

Transition

Situation: *Father said, I wasn't worth a hill of dried up beans.*

_____

Emotion of: *frustration* _____

What are the contributing factors of the emotion easy to use?

My father and I always got into arguments. I felt like I didn't measure up to him. He acted as if he didn't like me. _____

What are the new affirmations or belief systems that will transform this energy?

I love my father, and I now send love and light energy toward him and about him.

Situation: *I don't like what I'm doing for a living.*

Emotion of: *Dislike* _____

What are the contributing factors of this emotion?

I beat myself up all the time thinking I'm not good enough. It seems I'm always doing something wrong. I don't feel good about myself.

What are the new affirmations or belief systems that will transform this energy?

I know I am a part of God and a part of His genius creations. I will now honor that part of me. I will work to improve my health, my finances, my relationships, my spiritual well-being, and I'll develop a strong genius emotional base.

Use the genius value systems worksheets to reflect the transformations.

Reviewing

I recommend that you review the balancing chart several times a month and watch the changes you've selected in the emotions. If you're not experiencing any changes, it simply means the ego mind is still in charge, and you're not letting go of old conditions and emotions.

To do an analysis redo the graph chart.

Type of negative emotion   [1st week] [3rd week]   **Transform into a positive emotion**

-10   -5   0   5   10

Dislike _____   Love _____

Name a person, place or thing associated with this emotion. *Going to work* _____

Situation: *I dislike what I'm doing on my job.* *My attitude is getting better.*_____

Remember the objective is to transform the emotions to the genius positive side of the chart.

Mind: Use this space if there's an illness:

_____

List the ego emotions you're experiencing.

_____

What are you putting into your body?

_____

_____

Associated value systems:

_____

Type of negative emotion   **Transform into positive emotion**

-10   -5   0   5   10

_____   _____

Name a person, place, or thing associated with this emotion.

_____

Situation: _____

Type of negative emotion   Transform into positive emotion

-10   -5   0   5   10

_____   _____

Name a person, place, or thing associated with this emotion.

_____

Situation: _____

-10   -5   0   5   10

_____   _____

Name a person, place, or thing associated with this emotion.

_____

Situation:

_____

-10   -5   0   5   10

_____   _____

Name a person, place, or thing associated with this emotion.

_____

Situation:

_____

Transition

Situation:

_____

Emotion of _____

What are the contributing factors of this emotion?

_____

_____

_____

_____

What are the new affirmations or belief systems that will transform this energy?

_____

_____

_____

Emotion of _____

What are the contributing factors of this emotion?

_____

_____

_____

What are the new affirmations or belief systems that will transform this energy?

_____

_____

_____

Emotion of _____

What are the contributing factors of this emotion?

_____

_____

_____

What are the new affirmations or belief systems that will transform this energy?

_____

_____

_____

_____

Emotion of _____

What are the contributing factors of this emotion?

_____

_____

_____

_____

What are the new affirmations or belief systems that will transform this energy?

_____

_____

_____

_____

Sign and Date: _____

CHAPTER 8

THINGS I DESIRE

We can desire wonderful things in our lives. One of the ways to do this is to change our focus, remove all the undesirables in our lives, and replace them with the desirables. This exercise is a ritual that can transform unwanted desires into wonderful, desirable conditions. The ritual is a burning ritual of the undesirable conditions in each of the value systems. Also, you will define the desirable conditions you now want in your life.

Imagine that you are gifted with a healthy mind and body. You are in harmony with all your family members. You have an abundance of cash on hand to do whatever you want. You are in a position to help people at every social level. You live in your best imagined environment, have the career you're passionate about, and have the spiritual understanding of why you are here on Earth at this time.

This is your desirable list and it now becomes your focus in each of your value systems. For your challenging goals, build plans and action items for achieving them. Seek professional help and do your research when you need more information. Also, be sure to include in your meditations the main value system you're focused on.

Instructions:

1. Each value system is divided into sections. Use scrap paper for your undesirable lists. To start, select one value system to work through for the undesirables. Each value system will have a total of ten undesirable items. For now, make only a maximum of ten undesirables in each value system.

2. Make a list of one to ten of your major undesirables in a specific value system. You can make statements like, "I no longer desire _____," or "My undesirable is _____," or "I no longer desire _____ in my life."

Example:

Undesirables to Desirables—Health Values

List up to ten undesirables in your health values:

1. I desire to remove (*whatever illness*) out of my life.
2. I desire to remove unhealthy foods out of my body.
3. I desire to remove cigarettes out of my life!

3. Upon completing your undesirable list, go to your desirable page and create the opposite equivalent of your undesirables. The new desires will become your new affirmations. Use statements like: "I desire to love my wife." "I desire $20,000 a month income." "I desire a normal 20/20 vision." Be specific about your desires.

4. Once you have established your desirable list, create a ritual in which physically burn the paper on which you have written your undesirables. As the paper is burning, you can make statements like, "I now release these conditions to no longer be a part of my life." "From this day forward, I no longer give these conditions any attention."

5. Now the focus and intention are on your desirable list. Create a ritual. For example: Say each desirable affirmation in front of a mirror looking directly into your eyes. Do your rituals every day until you begin to see signs of the desirable manifesting!

Things I Desire—Health Values

List up to ten desirables in your health values:

1. I desire to heal, uplift, and purify my mind and body.
2. I desire to eat and drink wholesome foods.
3. I am in control of what I put in my mind and body.

6. Create a creed using the five Ds (see below) to generate an energy field around your desirables.

7. When your feelings are strong, follow the same routine for the other value systems.

+ **Desire:** When you desire something, your sense of longing is excited by the enjoyment or the thought of the desire, and you want to take actions to obtain your goal.

+ **Determination:** This quality makes you continue to do or achieve something difficult.

+ **Discipline:** This way of behaving shows a willingness to obey rules or orders.

+ **Dedication:** A feeling of strong support for or loyalty to something is the quality or state of being dedicated to a person, group, cause, etc.

+ **Detachment:** This is the act or process of separating something from a larger thing.

Example affirmation: I am *disciplined* to create the things I *desire* in life. I have the *determination* to complete all the things I love to do with excitement and *dedication*. I have the *discipline* to *detach* myself from any undesirable conditions I may have created.

My creed for desires

UNDESIRABLES TO DESIRABLES—HEALTH VALUES

List up to ten undesirables in your Health values:

1. _____

_____

_____

2. _____

_____

_____

3. _____

_____

_____

4. _____

_____

_____

5. _____

_____

_____

6. _____

_____

_____

7. _____

_____

_____

8. _____

_____

_____

9. _____

_____

_____

10. _____

_____

_____

Make your equivalent desire list before the symbolic burning.

THINGS I DESIRE—HEALTH VALUES

List up to ten desirables in your Health values:

1. _____

_____

_____

2. _____

_____

_____

3. _____

_____

_____

4. _____

_____

5. _____

6. _____

7. _____

8. _____

9. _____

10. _____

What are my first steps toward my new Health desires?

1. _____

_____

2. _____

_____

_____

_____

3. _____

_____

_____

_____

UNDESIRABLES TO DESIRABLES—CAREER AND PERSONAL VALUES

List up to ten undesirables in your Career and Personal values:

1. _____

   _____

   _____

2. _____

   _____

   _____

3. _____

   _____

   _____

4. _____

   _____

   _____

5. _____

   _____

   _____

6. _____

   _____

   _____

7. _____

   _____

8. _____

9. _____

10. _____

Make your equivalent desire list before the symbolic burning.

THINGS I DESIRE—CAREER AND PERSONAL VALUES

List up to ten desirables in your Career and Personal values:

1. _____

2. _____

3. _____

4. _____

5. _____

6. _____

7. _____

8. _____

9. _____

10. _____

What are my first steps toward my new Career and Personal development desires?

1. _____

_____

_____

2. _____

_____

_____

_____

3. _____

_____

_____

_____

UNDESIRABLES TO DESIRABLES—EMOTIONAL VALUES

List up to ten undesirables in your Emotional values:

1. _____

   _____

   _____

2. _____

   _____

   _____

3. _____

   _____

   _____

4. _____

   _____

   _____

5. _____

   _____

   _____

6. _____

   _____

   _____

7. _____

   _____

8. _____

_____

_____

9. _____

_____

_____

10. _____

_____

_____

Make your equivalent desire list before the symbolic burning.

THINGS I DESIRE—EMOTIONAL VALUES

List up to ten desirables in your Emotional values:

1. _____

_____

_____

2. _____

_____

_____

3. _____

_____

_____

4. _____

5. _____

6. _____

7. _____

8. _____

9. _____

10. _____

What are my first steps toward my new emotional desires?

1. _____

_____

_____

2. _____

_____

_____

_____

3. _____

_____

_____

_____

UNDESIRABLES TO DESIRABLES—FAMILY VALUES

List up to ten undesirables in your Family values:

1. _____

   _____

   _____

2. _____

   _____

   _____

3. _____

   _____

   _____

4. _____

   _____

   _____

5. _____

   _____

   _____

6. _____

   _____

   _____

7. _____

   _____

   _____

8. _____

_____

_____

9. _____

_____

_____

10. _____

_____

_____

Make your equivalent desire list before the symbolic burning.

Things I Desire—Family Values

List up to ten desirables in your Family values:

1. _____

_____

_____

2. _____

_____

_____

3. _____

_____

_____

4. _____

_____

5. _____

6. _____

7. _____

8. _____

9. _____

10. _____

What are my first steps toward my new family desires?

1. _____

2. _____

_____

_____

_____

_____

3. _____

_____

_____

_____

UNDESIRABLES TO DESIRABLES—FINANCIAL VALUES

List up to ten undesirables in your Financial values:

1. _____

_____

_____

2. _____

_____

_____

3. _____

_____

_____

4. _____

_____

_____

5. _____

_____

_____

6. _____

_____

_____

7. _____

_____

8. _____

9. _____

10. _____

Make your equivalent desire list before the symbolic burning.

THINGS I DESIRE—FINANCIAL VALUES

List up to ten desirables in your Financial values:

1. _____

2. _____

3. _____

4. _____

5. _____

6. _____

7. _____

8. _____

9. _____

10. _____

What are my first steps toward my new financial desires?

1. _____

_____

_____

2. _____

_____

_____

_____

3. _____

_____

_____

_____

UNDESIRABLES TO DESIRABLES—PHYSICAL VALUES

List up to ten undesirables in your Physical values:

1. _____

   _____

   _____

2. _____

   _____

   _____

3. _____

   _____

   _____

4. _____

   _____

   _____

5. _____

   _____

   _____

6. _____

   _____

   _____

7. _____

   _____

8. _____

9. _____

10. _____

Make your equivalent desire list before the symbolic burning.

THINGS I DESIRE—PHYSICAL VALUES

List up to ten desirables in your Physical values:

1. _____

2. _____

3. _____

4. _____

5. _____

_____

6. _____

_____

7. _____

_____

8. _____

_____

9. _____

_____

10. _____

_____

What are my first steps toward my new physical desires?

1. _____

_____

2. _____

3. _____

UNDESIRABLES TO DESIRABLES—SOCIAL VALUES

List up to ten undesirables in your Social values:

1. _____

   _____

   _____

2. _____

   _____

   _____

3. _____

   _____

   _____

4. _____

   _____

   _____

5. _____

   _____

   _____

6. _____

   _____

   _____

7. _____

   _____

8. _____

9. _____

10. _____

Make your equivalent desire list before the symbolic burning.

THINGS I DESIRE—SOCIAL VALUES

List up to ten desirables in your Social values:

1. _____

2. _____

3. _____

4. _____

5. _____

6. _____

7. _____

8. _____

9. _____

10. _____

What are my first steps toward my new social desires?

1. _____

_____

_____

2. _____

_____

_____

_____

3. _____

_____

_____

_____

UNDESIRABLES TO DESIRABLES—SPIRITUAL VALUES

List up to ten undesirables in your Spiritual values:

1. _____

   _____

   _____

2. _____

   _____

   _____

3. _____

   _____

   _____

4. _____

   _____

   _____

5. _____

   _____

   _____

6. _____

   _____

   _____

7. _____

   _____

8. _____

_____

_____

9. _____

_____

_____

10. _____

_____

_____

Make your equivalent desire list before the symbolic burning.

THINGS I DESIRE—SPIRITUAL VALUES

List up to ten desirables in your Spiritual values:

1. _____

_____

_____

2. _____

_____

_____

3. _____

_____

_____

4. _____

5. _____

6. _____

7. _____

8. _____

9. _____

10. _____

What are my first steps toward my new Spiritual desires?

1. _____

2. _____

   _____

   _____

   _____

   _____

3. _____

   _____

   _____

   _____

Sign and Date: _____

FINAL SUMMARY

You are greater than you think you are. To know this great truth is to recognize your genius! A genius is something you are, and it is something you develop to be in this lifetime. We were born with everything intact, and everything is still intact. The difference we experience between the time we are born and now is caused by the fact that we were introduced to duality when we came to planet Earth, and as we grew, we forgot who we truly are. Every one of us can bring wonderful things to our planet or serve for a great cause bigger than ourselves.

We do this by organizing our thoughts, emotions, and beliefs. We build plans based on our highest values in life. I'm sure by now you know you've been on a journey all your life, and it won't end unless you want it to end. Even if you wanted the journey to end in this life, that would be a journey. The journey represents your life on our planet Earth.

The creativity processes ranges from thoughts (the thinker) to emotions (the feeler) to beliefs (the believer). *Create feelings about your new exciting direction and turn them into genius emotions.* With your thoughts, build on your new direction and create excitement. The believer has the crown because the believer has a connection with spirit. *It is what you believe that you will manifest!*

The discovery processes progress from beliefs to emotions to thoughts. The believer is the top tier of the subconscious mind, and the emotions come through the loudest. Emotions release energy out into the world. An aware thinker has a relationship with his or her spirit (spiritual). Be aware; the spirit knows there's cleanup to do in the subconscious mind to remove ego thinking, emotions, and belief systems. The cleanup is a spiritual event.

Learning how to live your life by your highest excitements and highest values is a worthy goal. The tools in *A Journey into Value Systems: Cracking the Genius Code* are powerful, and they work because their basic principles help you to recognize when you are in our genius or ego mind. When you apply the principles regularly, you will see dramatic changes in your values and belief systems. They are tools you can use every day to continue growth in all your value systems and genius work.

Learning to live by your highest excitements is genius work. The genius work comes in knowing where your emotions are at every moment. Emotion represents energy in motion. It is genius work in finding core beliefs that are manifesting unwanted situations and physical conditions in your life. Discovering and identifying when the ego mind has manifested a situation in your life is a big deal. Know you are allowed to change and create new genius emotions, value systems, and core belief systems.

The ego mind can experience excitement; however, the excitement will be destructive in some way. The ego's excitement will have a negative effect throughout your value systems, your environment; it will prove destructive to you or someone else. To avoid this mishap or if you have any doubt about what you're doing, the question to ask: What is my intent and purpose for taking this action? Use the feeler to recognize the upcoming emotions. You will know right away if the event is the highest and best for you to experience and if it is ego generated.

This journey requires getting rid of old, outdated beliefs. Many of us have beliefs we're not even aware of. Many times, those beliefs are what holds us back from many wonderful adventures. It is important to continually update your beliefs until you're having the time of your life.

There will be some value systems operating in the negative. Some value systems will be neutral. And others will be in the positive. The chapter Connecting to the Eight Elements will clearly define this through the chart at the beginning of each value system. If the ego mind mostly controls a value system, identify the value system as challenged. Be sure to identify where each of your value systems is at any given time. If a value system is operating in the negative, work on it immediately. Use the tools in the workbook to transform any negative beliefs operating within that value system.

From my observation (being the observer), everything seems to point back to love I am learning to connect with this love energy with and become one with it. I learned that love isn't my creation; rather, love is something I connect my mind and body to and become one with. When I learned this, I found it so much easier to bring this radiant energy into my mind and body. I am learning to feel it. I am learning to be a part of it. I am learning that love has a direct connection with all laws of the Universe such as the law of attraction and the law of abundance. I am learning that love has the power to heal the body, to heal the mind, to heal nations, and to heal the world.

I believe everyone has been given the key to access this love, and it is as simple as asking for this Universal Love. I believe love is the pathway of accessing your genius code. Only you can crack your genius code. No one else!

We are greater than we think we are! Connect to love, travel into the unknown, discover your highest values, create excitements, and crack your genius code.

Keith Reginald Thompson

BIBLIOGRAPHY

D. J. Demartini quotes. AZ Quotes. https://www.azquotes.com/quote/532030%20 Accessed August 5, 2019.

Dispenza, D. J. *Becoming Supernatural: How Common People are Doing the Uncommon.* Connecticut: Hay House, 2019.

Albert Einstein quotes. Quote Investigator. https://quoteinvestigator.com/2013/04/06/fish-climb/ Accessed August 5, 2016.

Haanel, C. *The Master Key System.* United States: Psychology Publishing, 1916.

Hay, Louise L. *Heal Your Body.* Carlsbad: Hay House, Inc., 1987

Lipton, B. "Understanding the Conscious & Subconscious Mind." Fractal Enlightenment https://fractalenlightenment.com/32650/life/understanding-the-conscious-subconscious-mind-with-bruce-lipton Accessed August 7, 2019.

Lipton, D. B. "Are You Programmed at Birth?" You Can Heal Your Life. August 17, 2010. https://www.healyourlife.com/are-you-programmed-at-birth

Murphy, D. J. *The Power of Your Subconscious Mind.* New Jersey: Prentice Hall PRT, 1962.

Peck, S. *The Road Less Traveled.* New York: Simon & Schuster, 1978.

Plano, Catherine. *The Magic of Thinking BIG.* 19 June 2019. https://www.catherineplano.com.au/magic-thinking-big/.

Rohn, J. "Protect the Mind." Top Results Academy. https://topresultsacademy.com/mind/protect/stand-guard/ Accessed August 7, 2019.

Rohn J. quotes. Brainy Quote https://www.brainyquote.com/citation/quotes/jim_rohn_165075 Accessed August 5, 2019.

Wattles, Wallace D. *The Science of Getting Rich.* Holyoke, Massachusetts: Elizabeth Towne Publishing, 1910.

Wilde, Stuart. *The Complete Guide Book To The Law of Attraction.* 23 May 2014. https://www.youtube.com/watch?v=O3JPHfBPr8A&t=4300s.